Psychiatric Patient Violence

Psychiatric Patient Violence

RISK & RESPONSE

Edited by
John Crichton

Duckworth

First published in 1995 by
Gerald Duckworth & Co. Ltd.
The Old Piano Factory
48 Hoxton Square, London N1 6PB
Tel: 071 729 5986
Fax: 071 729 0015

A catalogue record for this book is available
from the British Library

ISBN 0 7156 2661 2

Acknowledgments

The editor gratefully acknowledges the help and advice of Professor Elaine Murphy, Professor Herschel Prins, Dr Gordon Langley and Dr Adrian Grounds in the preparation of Chapters 2, 3 and 6. The advice and support of Dr Anne-Marie Crichton, the secretarial help of Mrs Maureen Fry and the assistance of Mrs Wendy Roberts, of Cambridge University Medical Library, are also much appreciated.

Typeset by Ray Davies
Printed in Great Britain by
Redwood Books Limited, Trowbridge

Contents

v

Contents

Contributors

Sir Louis Blom-Cooper QC. Chairman of the Mental Health Act Commission 1987-94.

Lorraine Conlon. Senior Nurse, The Reaside Clinic, Birmingham.

John Crichton. Nightingale Researcher Trinity Hall and Institute of Criminology, Cambridge University. Honorary Registrar in Psychiatry, Addenbrooke's Hospital NHS Trust.

Andrew Gage. Unit Manager, The Reaside Clinic, Birmingham.

Adrian Grounds. University Lecturer, Institute of Criminology, Cambridge University. Honorary Consultant Forensic Psychiatrist, Addenbrooke's Hospital NHS Trust.

Helen Hally. Director of Nursing, Riverside Mental Health Trust.

Tony Hillis. Director of Nursing and Operational Services, The Reaside Clinic, Birmingham.

Elaine Murphy. Vice-Chairman of the Mental Health Act Commission 1987-94. Professor of Old Age Psychiatry, United Medical and Dental Schools, Guy's Hospital.

Jonathan Potts. Head of C3 division, the Home Office.

Genevra Richardson. Professor of Public Law, Queen Mary and Westfield College, University of London.

Liz Sayce. Policy director of the National Association for Mental Health, MIND.

Geoff Shepherd. Director of Research, Sainsbury Centre for Mental Health.

Abbreviations

CFPN	Community Forensic Psychiatric Nurse
DHSS	Department of Health and Social Security
DOH	Department of Health
ECT	Electro-Convulsive Therapy
ECHR	European Court of Human Rights
EE	Expressed Emotion
GBH	Grievous Bodily Harm
GP	General Practitioner
HMSO	Her Majesty's Stationery Office
MHA	Mental Health Act
MHAC	Mental Health Act Commission
MHRT	Mental Health Review Tribunal
MIND	The National Association for Mental Health
NHS	National Health Service
NHS Exec.	National Health Service Executive
NLS patients	New Long Stay patients
POA	Prison Officers Association
prn	*pro re nata* (medication taken 'as required')
SDHT	South Devon Healthcare Trust
SHSA	Special Hospitals Service Authority

1

Introduction

*Louis Blom-Cooper, Helen Hally
and Elaine Murphy*

Georgina Robinson, an occupational therapist at the Edith Morgan Centre, Torquay, was fatally wounded by a patient on 1 September 1993. Having concluded a review of the mental health services of the South Devon Healthcare Trust early in 1994, we were invited by the Trust to conduct a public inquiry into the circumstances of her death. At an early point we decided that it would be helpful to invite a group of expert witnesses to address some of the issues which the Inquiry would be raising. We decided to have a seminar day to which experts in the mental health system, together with senior academics, representatives from the Royal Colleges, and senior civil servants, would be invited to speak, and others to contribute to the floor discussion. Two of us (L.B-C. and E.M.) had experience in tacking on to a public inquiry seminars, on selected topics, when we were involved in the Ashworth Hospital Inquiry in 1992. That, we concluded, had been a notable success in providing material which greatly informed the ultimate report. We decided to repeat the experience in a more modest way.

The seminar day was held in Newton Abbot on 1 August 1994. In style it was somewhere between an academic seminar and a public inquiry. There was lively discussion. We were pleased that many relatives of those involved and employees of the South Devon Healthcare Trust attended and made a significant contribution. The main object of the exercise was to inform the Inquiry team as we prepared our report and recommendations.

We were conscious, however, that the quality of the contributions from the main speakers was such that their papers should be presented in book form. Here then is that book

To help arrange the seminar day and the preparation of this volume we seconded Dr John Crichton, Nightingale Researcher from Trinity Hall Cambridge. We are most grateful to the trustees of the Nightingale Bequest for releasing Dr Crichton, whose post is in memory of Michael Nightingale, distinguished former member of Trinity Hall, and we owe a sincere debt of gratitude to him. Not only did he persuade busy practitioners to contribute to the seminar day, but he also edited this book, attended all the public hearings, and was of great assistance to us as a sounding board for many of our ideas.

There emerged three themes of particular interest which go to form the three sections of the book: psychiatric inpatient violence; managing the risk of violence, especially in those with a past history of it; and the response to patient violence.

Inpatient violence

Georgina Robinson was fatally wounded by an inpatient in hospital. We asked Dr Crichton to review the literature about hospital inpatient violence, particularly in Britain. This review is contained in Chapter 2. There emerges a picture of increasing violence in recent years within British psychiatric hospitals, although the rate of serious violence remains mercifully low.

Managing the risk of violence

Secondly, Georgina Robinson's assailant, Andrew Robinson (no relation), had a history of extremely serious violence when psychotically unwell, such that he had been detained in Broadmoor maximum security hospital and subject to special restrictions after his discharge. Given the oft quoted wisdom that nothing predicts future violence better than past violence, we asked two of our expert witnesses to address this question: When

2

should levels of control and supervision be reduced for someone with a record of violence?

In Chapter 3 Dr Crichton sets the scene and comments on present knowledge about predicting patient violence and the shift of current good practice away from a position where there can be a one-off decision about a patient's dangerousness, towards a continuing process of risk management.

We could have no more suitable opinion than that of Mr Jonathan Potts, head of C3 Division, the Home Office, author of Chapter 4. His department is responsible for the Home Office's role in the discharge of offender-patients whose crime has been so serious that when Crown Court judges are persuaded that a hospital order is an appropriate disposal, they feel compelled to add a restriction order, unlimited in time, under Section 41 of the Mental Health Act 1983. We are grateful to the Secretary of State for Home Affairs for allowing Mr Potts to contribute. His chapter should be required reading for those involved in the treatment of Restriction Order patients and for members of Mental Health Review Tribunals, who have the power to lift such orders, as was the case with Andrew Robinson in September 1986.

In Chapter 5 Dr Adrian Grounds approaches the same question but from the position of a psychiatrist in the field, currently supervising patients in the community who have committed violence in the past. His clinical wisdom steadfastly reinforces the point that risk management must be founded in good clinical history and not on a clinician's hunches or 'gut reactions'. Chillingly, he also reminds us that such risk always carries the possibility of disaster.

The Response to Psychiatric Patient Violence

Throughout the Inquiry we were struck, not only by the distress of Georgina Robinson's family, but also by that of the other Robinson family, Andrew's. One aspect of Andrew's illness that caused great difficulty over the years was the aggressive and threatening acts he committed when unwell. Our final theme was to look broadly at issues of response to patient violence.

In Chapter 6 Dr Crichton sets the scene and raises a variety of challenging points: Is there a place for discipline and sanctions within hospital over patients? When should patients be prosecuted for criminal acts? What care should be provided for the victims of assault? He concludes that there has been a shift of interest in the public's concern about psychiatry away from anxiety about over-control and abuses within institutions towards concern about under-control in the community. He argues for a balance of control which respects an individual's autonomy and also meets public concern over safety.

The contribution from senior nurses and managers from the Reaside Clinic (Chapter 7) approaches the problem of potentially violent patients from the perspective of those managing a medium secure unit where most of the patients have a past history of violent acts. Their contribution was refreshing in the optimism it engendered on the seminar day, which is reflected in their chapter. Violent patients are often unpopular and do not receive the treatment they deserve. The Reaside Clinic chapter describes how positive and novel practices have worked to produce and sustain a therapeutic environment, which has also reduced the risk of serious assault to its staff.

Professor Genevra Richardson's contribution (Chapter 8) is also novel and challenging although again from a different perspective and looking at a different aspect of the problem. She explores the possibility of a formal disciplinary framework over patients, particularly for those within maximum security. Many of her points accord with those of Dr Crichton, though she draws slightly different conclusions. She confessed on the seminar day to feeling a bit like a 'stalking horse' for these ideas. It is very clear from reading her proposals that the interests and welfare of patients are central and that formal disciplinary procedures are intended to replace *ad hoc* discipline which already exists without regulation, checks and balances. At the heart of her proposals there is the aim of furthering patient rights, while placing the problem of discipline in the real world, where misdemeanour caused by patients does exist and where staff must respond in a way which is not counter-therapeutic.

From yet another perspective Dr Geoff Shepherd (Chapter 9) looks at the problem of providing adequate community care for patients who tend to be violent in the community. His presentation struck many chords with our Inquiry. Effective teamwork and good communication between all professionals and carers involved was clearly something which would have benefited Andrew Robinson. Dr Shepherd's chapter provides invaluable advice on how a team should actually work together; his essay should be required reading for all in multidisciplinary teamwork. The points raised and suggested solutions about the care of 'new long-stay' or 'difficult to place' patients are similarly invaluable for anyone involved in planning community services.

The final chapter, by MIND's policy director Liz Sayce, provides an important balance to the contents of this volume: the user's perspective. She reminds us of the unbalanced debate within the media about psychiatric patient violence, and her suggestions for reform – her alternative '10-point plan' – outline many of the issues future mental health legislation must address.

Conclusions

It is all too easy for an Inquiry such as ours to be wise after the event and to shake to the foundations a service that has been found wanting. We have tried in our report, and in this volume, to be constructive. Perhaps the best tribute to the memory of Georgina Robinson is that lessons are learnt and that a better environment is created for patients and staff alike. In our Inquiry, and within the topics of the seminar day, we have not been afraid of addressing many thorny and difficult issues. The South Devon Healthcare Trust has had the courage to submit itself to the painful and expensive process of Public Inquiry. The Trust is already responding to the recommendations of our earlier review of mental health services, and we are confident that the lessons of the Inquiry, reflected in the report and in this volume of essays, will be appropriately learnt. This volume is intended to complement our Inquiry report in influencing better practice, not only in South Devon, but much more widely, so that future tragedy may be better avoided.

PART I

Inpatient Violence

A Review of Psychiatric Inpatient Violence

John Crichton

Violence and mental disorder

The relationship between violence and mental disorder is far from straightforward (Prins 1990), an initial problem being that different studies use different definitions of violence and mental disorder (discussed in Taylor 1993). In a recent review, Hodgins (1993) concludes that certain major mental disorders do increase the risk of criminal acts and violence. Monahan (1992a, 1993), a leading international authority in this field, has recently moved towards this position, marking a change from his previous view (Monahan & Steadman 1983).

It is perhaps of little comfort to the victims of violence that, contrary to the popular stereotype, the mentally disordered are rarely violent and even more rarely homicidal. Studies into the popular beliefs about mental disorder and violence include Fracchia *et al* (1976), Monahan (1992b), Olmstead & Durham (1976), Steadman (1981) and Steadman & Cocozza (1978). Gerber *et al* (1981) and Shain & Phillips (1991) comment on how the mentally disordered are portrayed in the media. Crichton (1993) describes a horror film, *Asylum*, in which every psychiatric patient featured has a history of homicide and their psychiatrist also becomes mentally unwell and kills.

Häfner & Böker (1982) studied all mentally abnormal offenders who had committed or attempted homicide in West Germany from 1955 to 1964. The group was responsible for 5% of these offences and at that time the prevalence of mental disorder in West Germany was 3%-5%. There were, however, important differences between diagnostic groups: the incidence of homicidal violence for schizophrenics was five per 10,000, with the risk of suicide 100 times greater than that of homicide; for those with affective disorder the rate of homicidal violence was six per 100,000, with the risk of suicide 1,000 times greater than that of homicide.

During the autumn of 1991 increased British public concern about homicides involving the mentally disordered prompted the setting up of the Confidential Inquiry into Homicides and Suicides of Mentally Disordered People (Boyd 1994). Over a period of eighteen months 100 cases of homicide were identified in which the offender was subsequently admitted to psychiatric hospital. Slightly confusingly, this eighteen-month period included homicides over three years, during which there were estimated to be 1,800-2,100 homicides in England and Wales. Of those 100 cases, 52 had a previous episode of mental disorder and 31 had previous criminal charges. Only 34 had contact with the psychiatric services during the twelve months before the homicide and of those in only 22 cases could full case details be examined. Of those 22 only one case involved a psychiatric inpatient, although nineteen were receiving outpatient care.

There remains the small proportion of psychiatric patients who are at risk of committing serious violence, and it is the responsibility of mental health services to predict and manage such violence as effectively as possible. Violence caused by the mentally disordered is concentrated within psychiatric hospitals partly because violent behaviour itself is an admission criterion, with studies estimating violence to others as preceding between one in ten and one in three admissions (Johnstone *et al* 1986, Lagos *et al* 1977, Tardiff & Sweillam 1980).

The Health Services Advisory Committee (1987) found that in Great Britain about a tenth of psychiatric inpatients commit violent assaults against staff and that NHS staff were three times more likely to suffer injury than industrial workers, mainly because of assault. Although violence towards *others* is the main theme discussed here, this cannot be entirely divorced from self harm and suicidal behaviour. The correlation between suicidal behaviour and violence is established epidemiologically (Holinger 1987) and observed clinically (Tardiff & Sweillam 1980). Apter *et al* (1991) studied the risk of suicide in non-violent and violent patients; finding that the violent group reported fewer feelings of sadness, they suggest that suicidal risk should be managed differently in highly violent patients.

Psychiatric inpatient violence

In review articles Haller & Deluty (1988) and Shah *et al* (1991) comment on the evidence that inpatient violence is increasing. This is supported by a number of studies: Adler *et al* (1983), Edwards *et al* (1988), James *et al* (1990), Noble & Roger (1989), Tardiff (1984) and Walker & Caplan (1993). Shah (1993) discusses whether there is a true increase in inpatient violence or whether this finding is an artifact caused by a greater awareness of violence generally and errors generated by comparing different types of study. Walker & Caplan (1993) compared psychiatric hospital assault rates and violent crime rates in two Health Authorities and found that the level of inpatient violence reflected the level of violence at large.

Publications about psychiatric inpatient violence have exploded in number, perhaps indicating an increase in anxiety amongst staff about assault as well as an increase in interest in the subject (Crichton 1995). Drinkwater (1982) observes that before the late 1970s there was only a handful of British papers on the subject. Shah (1993) observes that there have been over 100 international publications on the topic since 1980.

Table 1 summarises the main findings of British studies into inpatient violence. There are methodological differences, particularly in the definitions of violence used, which make comparisons between studies difficult. One major weakness of retrospective studies looking at standard incident forms is that they are likely to underestimate levels of violence (Lion *et al*

Table 1. Studies of British Psychiatric Inpatient Violence			
Authors	Location	Method	Definition of violence
Fottrell et al 1978	Large general psychiatric hospital over 39 weeks	Prospective reporting. Standard forms	Physical violence
Fottrell 1980	Hospital A: Large general psychiatric hospital over 52 weeks Hospital B: Large general psychiatric hospital over 16 weeks Hospital C: General psychiatric unit as part of a general hospital. 52 weeks	Prospective reporting Special forms. Spot checking etc Interviews with assailants and victims	1° * 2° 3° 1° * 2° 3° 1° * 2° 3°
Armond 1982	4 semi-secure wards in a general psychiatric hospital over between 6.5 and 39 weeks	Prospective reporting Standard forms Informal interview	Actual physical injury and deliberate property damage
Aiken 1984	17 bed secure ward in acute general psychiatric hospital over 26 weeks	Prospective reporting Special forms	Assault against staff causing actual harm
Hodgkinson et al (1985)	Large general psychiatric hospital over 104 weeks	Retrospective reporting Standard forms	Assaults on staff
Pearson et al (1986)	Large general psychiatric hospital over 52 weeks	Retrospective reporting Standard forms	Damage to property or injury to another person
Larkin et al (1988)	Maximum security hospital over 26 weeks	Prospective Special forms with checking	Behaviour which could cause damage to the patient, others or property
Coldwell & Naismith (1989)	20 bedded high dependency ward of a maximum security hospital over 52 weeks	Retrospect reporting of standard incident forms, study of ward reports and medical notes	Violent action to people and property excluding verbal aggression
Torpy & Hall (1993)	30 bedded medium secure unit over 156 weeks	Prospective reporting Standard forms	Physical violence
Walker & Seifert (1994)	6 bedded psychiatric intensive care unit over 26 weeks	Prospective reporting Special and standard forms	Physical assaults to another person
Kennedy et al (1995)	77 bedded medium secure unit over 203 weeks	Retrospective reporting Standard forms	An attack on property or assault involving physical contact

* The authors employ a version of Fottrell's 1980 classification of violence severity: 1° No physical injury; 2° Minor injury, e.g. bruises; 3° Major injury, e.g. large lacerations, fractures etc.

Table 1. (continued)

Numbers of incidents	Crude rate of violent incidents per patient per year	'Problem patients'	Other comments
69	0.07	14 patients cause 50.3% of incidents	
338 13 2 54 – – 32 1 1	0.32 0.15 0.61	3% of patients caused 70% incidents 4% of patients caused 59% of incidents 1% of patients caused 41% of incidents	Violent patients were more likely to have history of violence The only $3°$ incidents were suicide Incidents happened more frequently on acute wards
40	2.0	3 patients caused 50% of incidents	More incidents took place after changes to ward routine
* $1°$ 14 $2°$ 21 $3°$ 6	7.8	4 patients caused 56.1% of incidents	Violent patients had a significant history of violence
Year 1 274 Year 2 348	Unable to calculate from data in the paper	5% of violent patients caused 26% of incidents	77% of violent patients only involved in 1 or 2 incidents
* $1°$ 197 $2°$ 82 $3°$ 4	0.65	1 patient responsible for 12% of incidents	
1144 (31 life threatening)	3.9	4% of patients caused 60% of incidents	Male crude rate 1.4; female 12.0. Females comprising 25% of population; responsible for 75% of incidents
116	5.8†	19.3% of patients caused 62.1% of incidents	Marked seasonal variation with more incidents in winter
563 (2 life threatening)	7.9**	1 patient caused 8% of incidents	Virtually no violence in areas designed for occupation or therapy
* $1°$ 6 $2°$ 28 $3°$ 3	12.3†		More assaults from those with a history of drug abuse or a criminal record
* $1°$ 342 $2°$ 280 $3°$ 66	4.9	1 patient responsible for 6.4% of incidents	Seclusion found unnecessary in management of violence

†Crude rate of violent incidents per *bed* per year
**Rate calculated using additional data supplied by Dr. Torpy.

1981); another weakness of several studies is that the violent group of patients is investigated without comparison to the non-violent group. Several of the British studies look at severity of outcome from violence, using Fottrell's (1980) scale of severity of injury, but to use outcome as the measure of a violent act does not take account of the role of chance in determining the extent of any injury (Shah *et al* 1991; Larkin *et al* 1988).

Included in Table 1 is a crude rate of violence per patient per year, calculated from details, where available, about average bed occupancy rates. Although there are systematic errors in calculating these rates, they indicate that the highest rates of violence are in locked wards (Aiken 1984) and psychiatric intensive care units (Walker & Seifert 1994) of general psychiatric hospitals. This may be because inpatient violence is the main admission criterion for these units, which may also explain why the majority of patients there were repeatedly violent. The highest number of serious assaults however, are reported at Rampton maximum security hospital where there was found to be more than one life threatening episode of violence per week (Larkin *et al* 1988).

In an early international study Stierlin (1956) describes the findings of a questionnaire returned by 92 European psychiatric hospitals which reported, over an unspecified time period, 773 acts of aggression including sixteen deaths. Ekblom (1970) found a low incidence of violent acts within the Swedish hospital system; among 27,000 patients were found 27 serious assaults, eight of which were fatal. Other international studies include Cooper & Mendonca (1991), Depp (1976), Dooley (1986) and the individual studies included in Lion & Reid's edited work (1983). There is consensus between the British and these international studies that serious violence is rare, that most patients are not violent, and that a minority of 'problem patients' cause a disproportionately high number of incidents.

2. A Review of Psychiatric Inpatient Violence

The characteristics of violent inpatients

Diagnosis

Several studies suggest that the most sizeable group of violent patients consists of those with schizophrenia, but these studies fail to take into account the higher proportion of patients with schizophrenia found in hospital compared to patients with other diagnoses (Smith & McKay 1965; Fottrell 1980; Pearson *et al* 1986; Tardiff & Sweillam 1979). One study found that schizophrenics had the lowest rate of violence (Evenson *et al* 1974), and others found no difference in the rates between diagnostic groups (Torpy & Hall 1993; Tanke & Yesavage 1985). Hodgkinson *et al* 1985 found a higher rate of violence in personality disordered and schizophrenic patients in a young age range, while in those with organic diagnoses there was a greater rate of violence in an older age range.

Noble & Roger (1989) compared 137 inpatients who had committed assaults with matched inpatient controls. They found that inpatients who committed assaults were more likely to have schizophrenia and be *actively* psychotic.

Gender

Studies have tended to show either an equal rate of violence between the sexes (Noble & Roger 1989) or a greater rate of violence in female patients (Binder & McNiel 1990; Fottrell 1980; Larkin *et al* 1988; McKerricker *et al* 1966; Palmstierna & Wistedt; Rappeport & Lassen 1966). This finding is most marked in Larkin *et al*'s (1988) study at Rampton maximum security hospital, where women make up 25% of the patient population and were involved in 75% of the violent incidents. The factors behind the higher rate of female patient violence, particularly in a secure setting, may be shared with the factors associated with the higher rate of violence among female prisoners (Maden 1993): Dobash *et al* (1986) reports the rate of offences per 100 prisoners in 1985 was 335 for women and 160 for men. However, the factors behind the higher rate of violence among female prisoners remain uncertain.

Race

Only one study (Noble & Roger 1989), using a matched control approach, found a greater proportion of Afro-Caribbean patients were violent. These patients were also found to be younger, 'more psychotic', more seriously violent, more likely to be detained and more likely to be treated in a locked ward. One possible explanation for Noble & Roger's (1989) finding is either that, for Afro-Caribbean patients, violence is a more weighty admission criterion, or that the non-violent mentally disordered are less likely to be admitted within that racial group. There is no consensus on the relationship between inpatient violence and race.

Restriction order patients

Torpy and Hall (1993) found that patients who had been placed on a restriction order (Section 41 MHA 1983) by a Crown Court following a conviction for a grave offence, were no more likely to be assaultive than a non-restricted patient. A restriction order was not in itself found to be a good predictor of aggressive behaviour within hospital.

Victims of assault

There is no consensus about whether staff or patients are more commonly assaulted, both groups are common victims. One study (Hodgkinson *et al* 1985) found that inexperienced staff were assaulted more frequently, and another that inexperienced staff were more likely to be injured by assault (Carmel & Hunter 1989). Walker and Seifert (1994), however, found that trained staff were assaulted more frequently. Hodgkinson *et al* (1985) also found that a small group of staff were repeatedly assaulted and suggested this was either due to particular staff working in high risk areas, or because of individual staff styles. Some authors suggest that rigid or authoritarian staff are assaulted more often (Cooper & Mendonca 1989; Durivage 1989).

Depp (1976) reviewed 238 assaults on other patients, who did not hit back and required medical attention. Aggressors tended to have more physical handicaps than their victims and patients involved in repeated incidents tended to keep their role; victims were victims again and aggressors were aggressors again. Assaults occurred more frequently on mixed rather than single wards and men tended not to assault women or *vice versa*.

Antecedents of violence

In the only British study to look comprehensively at the antecedents of violence, Powell *et al* (1994) found that most commonly a high state of arousal preceded violence (in 31% of cases), a finding supported by Aiken (1984). Restrictions placed on patients (20.8%) and provocation by others (19%) also commonly preceded violence. Violence arising from staff members initiating contact with a patient was rare (0.01%).

Structural factors

Several studies suggest that violence is more common when there is little structured activity (Pearson *et al* 1986; Depp 1976; Fottrell 1980). Torpy & Hall (1993) found virtually no violence in areas designed for occupation or therapy. Drinkwater (1988) found that violent behaviour was four times higher during periods without planned activity.

One study reports a greater amount of violence when staff were busier (Adler *et al* 1983), and there has been some discussion about serious assaults occurring when staffing levels are poor (Martin 1984; Yates 1981). James *et al* (1990) and Fineberg *et al* (1988) report increases in violence to be strongly associated with the use of temporary staff. An observational study suggested that violence was more common in wards with poorly defined staff roles, 'weak' staff and an unpredictable ward programme (Katz & Kirkland 1990). There is agreement that within hospital fear, confusion and the under-occupation of patients breed violence (Katz & Kirkland 1990; Phillip & Nasr 1983; Depp 1976).

Future research

Several authors have suggested that future research into inpatient violence should develop actuarial or statistical techniques to improve prediction of which patients are likely to be violent (Haller & Deluty 1988; Shah *et al* 1991; Shah 1993). Palmsterna & Wistedt (1988) followed this approach using the Brief Psychiatric Rating Scale (Overall & Gorham 1962) and did not find it very helpful. The task of predicting patient violence at large has proved extremely difficult, and this is discussed in Chapter 3. There is no indication that actuarial or statistical approaches will be more successful in the inpatient setting. Stark *et al* (1994) are critical of such approaches and suggest that rather than relying on staff to identify high risk patients, hospital management should strive to create a safe environment, with the appropriate use of observation, alarm systems, staff support and training.

Crichton (1995) argues that it is insufficient to simply consider violence as a disease symptom and that the debate about inpatient violence should be placed within its legal context with consideration of what control and discipline it is reasonable to exercise over patients.

It is safe to conclude that concern over inpatient violence will continue to challenge psychiatric staff and health care planners. It can also be predicted that now awareness of patient violence has been heightened in society at large, studies will emerge describing the risk of assault to family and community carers. It is likely that such studies will concur with the main inpatient findings, that serious assault is rare, but minor assaults are common and continue to be a major problem.

References

ADLER W.N., KREEGER C. & ZEIGLER P. (1980) Patient violence in a private psychiatric ward. In J.R. Lion & W.H. Reid (eds) *Assaults within Psychiatric Facilities*. New York: Grune & Stratton.

AIKEN G.J.M. (1984) Assaults on staff in a locked ward: prediction and consequences. *Medicine, Science and the Law* 24 199-207.

APTER A., KOTLER M., SEVY S., PLUTCHIK R., BROWN S.L., FOSTER H., HILLBRAND M., KORN M.L. & VAN PRAAG H.M. (1991) Correlates of risk of suicide in violent and nonviolent psychiatric patients. *American Journal of Psychiatry* 148 883-7.

ARMOND A.D. (1982) Violence in the semi-secure ward of a psychiatric hospital. *Medicine, Science and the Law* 22 203-9.

BINDER L. & McNIEL E. (1990) The relationship of gender to violent behaviour in acutely disturbed psychiatric patients. *Journal of Clinical Psychiatry* 51 110-14.

BOYD W.D. (Director) (1994) *A Preliminary Report on Homicide*. London: The Steering Committee of the Confidential Inquiry into Homicides and Suicides by Mentally Ill People.

CARMEL H. & HUNTER M. (1989) Staff injuries from in-patient violence. *Hospital and Community Psychiatry* 40 41-6.

COLDWELL J.B. & NAISMITH L.J. (1989) Violent incidents on a special care ward of a special hospital. *Medicine, Science and the Law* 29 116-23.

COOPER A.J. & MENDONCA J.D. (1991) A prospective study of patient assaults on nurses in a provincial psychiatric hospital in Canada. *Acta Psychiatrica Scandinavica* 84 163-6.

CRICHTON J.H.M. (1993) A new look at *Asylum*. *Psychiatric Bulletin* 17 758-9.

CRICHTON J.H.M. (1995) Psychiatric in-patient violence: issues of English law and discipline. *Medicine, Science and the Law*. In press.

DEPP F.C. (1976) Violent behaviour patterns on psychiatric wards. *Aggressive Behaviour* 2 259-306.

DOBASH R.P., DOBASH R.E. & GUTTERIDGE S. (1986) *The Imprisonment of Women*. Oxford: Blackwell.

DOOLEY E. (1986) Aggressive behaviour in a secure hospital. *Medicine, Science and the Law* 26 125-30.

DRINKWATER J. (1982) Violence in psychiatric hospitals. In M.P. Feldman (ed.) *Developments in the Study of Criminal Behaviour*, vol II. Chichester: John Wiley & Sons.

DRINKWATER J. (1989) Violence in psychiatric hospitals. In K. Howells & C.R. Hollin (eds) *Clinical Approaches to Violence*. Chichester: John Wiley & Sons.

DRINKWATER J.M. (1988) *An Investigation of Psychiatric Ward Management and Violence.* Unpublished PhD thesis cited in Drinkwater (1989).

DURIVAGE A. (1989) Assaultive behaviour before it happens. *Canadian Journal of Psychiatry* **34** 393-7.

EDWARDS J.G., JONES D., REID W.H. & CHU C-C. (1988) Physical assaults on a psychiatric unit of a general hospital. *American Journal of Psychiatry* **145** 1568-71.

EKBLOM B. (1970) *Acts of Violence by Patients in Mental Hospitals.* Stockholm: Scandinavian University Press.

EVENSON R.C., SLETTEN I.W., ALTMAN H. & BROWN M.L. (1974) Disturbing behaviour, a study of incident reports. *Psychiatry Quarterly* **48** 266-75.

FINEBERG N.A., JAMES D.V. & SHAH A.K. (1988) Agency nurses and violence in a psychiatric ward. *The Lancet* i 474.

FOTTRELL E., BEWLEY T. & SQUIZZONI M.A. (1978) A study of aggressive and violent behaviour among a group of psychiatric inpatients. *Medicine, Science and the Law* **18** 66-9.

FOTTRELL E. (1980) A study of violent behaviour among patients in psychiatric hospitals. *British Journal of Psychiatry* **136** 216-21.

FRACCHIA J., CANALE D., CAMBRIA E., RUEST E. & SHEPPARD C. (1976) Public views of ex-mental patients: a note on perceived dangerousness and unpredictability. *Psychiatric Reports* **38** 495-8.

GERBER G., GROSS L., MORGAN M. & SIGNORIELLI N. (1981) Health and medicine on television. *New England Journal of Medicine* **305** 901-4.

HÄFNER H. & BÖKER W. (1982) *Crimes of Violence by Mentally Disordered Offenders* (tr. H. Marshall). Cambridge: Cambridge University Press (original work published in 1973).

HALLER R.M. & DELUTY R.H. (1988) Assaults on staff by psychiatric inpatients. *British Journal of Psychiatry* **152** 174-9.

HEALTH SERVICE ADVISORY COMMITTEE (1987) *Violence to Staff in the Health Service.* London: HMSO, Health and Safety Committees.

HODGINS S. (1993) The criminality of mentally disordered persons. In S. Hodgins (ed.) *Mental Disorder and Crime.* Newbury Park, California: Sage Publications, p. 16.

HODGKINSON P.E., McIVOR L. & PHILIPS M. (1985) Patient assaults on staff in a psychiatric hospital: a two-year retrospective study. *Medicine, Science and the Law* **25** 288-94.

HOLINGER P.C. (1987) *Violent Deaths in the United States.* New York: Guilford Press.

JAMES D.V., FINEBERG N.A., SHAH A.K. & PRIEST R.G. (1990) An increase in violence on an acute psychiatric ward – a study of associated factors. *British Journal of Psychiatry* **156** 846-52.

JOHNSTONE E.C., CROW T.J., JOHNSON A.L. & MACMILLAN J.F. (1986) The Northwick Park study of first episodes of schizophrenia. 1.

Presentation of the illness and procedure relating to admission. *British Journal of Psychiatry* **148** 115-20.

KATZ P. & KIRKLAND F.R. (1990) Violence and social structure on mental hospital wards *Psychiatry* **53** 262-76.

KENNEDY J., HARRISON J., HILLIS T. & BLUGLASS R. (1995) Analysis of violent incidents in a regional secure unit. *Medicine, Science and the Law*. In press.

LARKIN E., MURTAGH S. & JONES S. (1988) A preliminary study of violent incidents in a special hospital (Rampton). *British Journal of Psychiatry* **153** 226-31.

LAGOS J.M., PERLMUTTER K. & SAEXINGER H. (1977) Fear of the mentally ill: empirical support for the common man's response. *American Journal of Psychiatry* **134** 1134-7.

LION J.R., SNYDER W.& MERRIL G.L. (1981) Underreporting of assaults on staff at a state hospital. *Hospital and Community Psychiatry* **32** 497-8.

LION J.R. & REID W.H. (1983) *Assaults within psychiatric facilities*. Orlando: Grune & Stratton.

McKERRACHER D.W., STREET D.R.K. & SEGAL L.J. (1966) A comparison of the behaviour problems presented by male and female sub-normal offenders. *British Journal of Psychiatry* **112** 891-7.

MADEN T. (1993) Women as violent offenders and violent patients. In P.J. Taylor (ed.) *Violence in Society*. London: The Royal College of Physicians.

MARTIN J.P. (1984) *Hospitals in Trouble*. Oxford: Blackwell, p. 103.

MONAHAN J. & STEADMAN H. (1983) Crime and mental disorder: an epidemiological approach. In M. Tonry & N. Morris (eds) *Crime and Justice: An Annual Review of Research* (Vol. 4 pp. 145-89). Chicago: University of Chigaco Press.

MONAHAN J. (1992a) Mental disorder and violent behaviour. *American Psychological Association* **47** 1-11.

MONAHAN J. (1992b) Mental disorder and violent behaviour: perceptions and evidence. *American Psychologist* **47** 511-21.

MONAHAN J. (1993) Mental disorder and violence: another look. In S. Hodgins (ed.) *Mental Disorder and Crime*. Newbury Park, California: Sage Publications.

NOBLE P. & ROGER S. (1989) Violence by psychiatric inpatients. *British Journal of Psychiatry* **155** 384-90.

OLMSTEAD D.W. & DURHAM K. (1976) Stability of mental health attitudes: a semantic differential study. *Journal of Health and Social Behaviour* **17** 35-44.

OVERALL J. & GORHAM D.R. (1962) The brief psychiatric rating scale. *Psychological Rep.* **10** 799-812.

PALMSTIERNA T. & WISTEDT B. (1988) Prevalence of risk factors for aggressive behaviour and characteristics of an involuntary admitted population. *Acta Psychiatrica Scandinavica* **78** 227-9.

PEARSON M., WILMOT E. & PADI M. (1986) A study of violent behaviour among in-patients in a psychiatric hospital. *British Journal of Psychiatry* **149** 232-5.

PHILLIPS P. & NASR S.J. (1983) Seclusion and restraint and prediction of violence. *American Journal of Psychiatry* **140** 229-32.

POWELL G., CAAN W. & CROWE M. (1994) What events precede violent incidents in psychiatric hospitals? *British Journal of Psychiatry* **165** 107-12.

PRINS H. (1990) Mental abnormality and criminality – an uncertain relationship. *Medicine, Science and the Law* **30** 247-57.

RAPPEPORT J.R. & LASSEN G. (1966) The dangerousness of female patients, a comparison of the arrest rate of discharged psychiatric patients and the general population. *American Journal of Psychiatry* **123** 413-19.

SHAH A.K. (1993) An increase in violence among psychiatric inpatients: real or apparent? *Medicine, Science and the Law* **33** 227-30.

SHAH A.K., FINEBERG N.A. & JAMES D.V. (1991) Violence among psychiatric inpatients. *Acta Psychiatrica Scandinavica* **84** 305-9.

SHAIN R. & PHILLIPS J. (1991) The stigma of mental illness: labelling and stereotyping in the news. In L. Wilkins & P. Patterson (eds) *Risky Business: Communicating issues of science, risk and public policy*. Westport CT: Greenwood Press, pp. 61-74.

SMITH C.M. & McKAY L. (1965) The open psychiatric ward and its vicissitudes. *American Journal of Psychiatry* **121** 763-7.

STARK C., FARRAR H. & KIDD B. (1994) Violence in psychiatric units. *British Journal of Psychiatry* **165** 554.

STEADMAN H. (1981) Critically reassessing the accuracy of public perceptions of the dangerousness of the mentally ill. *Journal of Health and Social Behaviour* **22** 310-16.

STEADMAN H.J. & COCOZZA J.J. (1978) Selective reporting and the public's misconceptions of the criminally insane. *Public Opinion Quarterly* **41** 523-33.

STIERLIN H. (1956) Der gewalttätige Patient. *Bibl. psychiat. neurol.* **97** 1-62.

TANKE E.D. & YESAVAGE J.A. (1985) Characteristics of assaultive patients who do not provide visible cues of potential violence. *American Journal of Psychiatry* **142** 1409-13.

TARDIFF K. & SWEILLAM A. (1980) Assault, suicide and mental illness. *Archives of General Psychiatry* **37** 164-9.

TAYLOR P.J. (1993) Mental illness and violence. In P.J. Taylor (ed.) *Violence in Society*. London: The Royal College of Physicians, p. 85.

TORPY D. & HALL M. (1993) Violent incidents in a secure unit. *Journal of Forensic Psychiatry* **4** 517-44.

2. A Review of Psychiatric Inpatient Violence

WALKER W.D. & CAPLAN R.P. (1993) Assaultive behaviour in acute psychiatric wards and its relationship to violence in the community: a comparison of two health districts. *Medicine, Science and the Law* **33** 300-4.

WALKER Z. & SEIFERT R. (1994) Violent incidents in a psychiatric intensive care unit. *British Journal of Psychiatry* **164** 826-8.

YATES J. (1981) Staff-patient ratios and hospital enquiries. *Nursing Times* **26** 2143-5.

PART II

Managing the Risk of Violence

The Prediction of Psychiatric Patient Violence

John Crichton

Prediction of violence

The need to try to predict violence has been with psychiatry for some time. Neither statistical models nor clinical skills have yet proved reliable predictors of future violence (Scott 1977; Cocozza & Steadman 1976; Lidz *et al* 1993; Litwick *et al* 1993). Monahan (1988) summarised the following conclusions about dangerousness and mental disorder:

(1) The upper bound of accuracy that even the best risk assessment technology could achieve was in the order of .33. In other words, for each mentally disordered patient predicted to be violent two will not be.

(2) The best demographic predictors of violence amongst the mentally disordered are the same for the non-mentally disordered (i.e. age, gender, social class, substance abuse and history of violence).

(3) The poorest predicting factors amongst the mentally disordered are diagnosis, severity of disorder and personality traits.

There is robust evidence, however, that *active* psychotic symptoms are associated with an increased risk of violence (Swanson *et al* 1990; Link *et al* 1992). Monahan (1993) comments on the importance of these studies:

The data independently reported by Swanson *et al* (1990) and Link *et al* (1992) are remarkable and provide the crucial missing element that begins to fill out the epidemiological picture of mental disorder and violence. Together, these two studies suggest that the currently mentally disordered – those actively experiencing serious psychotic symptoms – are involved in violent behavior at rates several times those of non-disordered members of the general population, and that this difference persists even when a wide array of demographic and social factors are taken into consideration.

Monahan (1988) also made four specific criticisms about studies into prediction of dangerousness:

- that the range of predictor variables has been too narrow;
- that research tools for measurement of violence have been weak;
- that samples of patients studied have been too restrictive;
- that research efforts have been fragmented and lack coordination.

The MacArthur Risk Assessment study (Steadman *et al* 1993), currently under way in the United States, specifically addresses these criticisms and aims in a comprehensive large research programme to identify the risk factors and cues to violent behaviour among the mentally disordered. In particular there is interest in the situational and contextual factors behind violence. Steadman *et al* (1993) suggest five factors that may be risk markers for violence and which are worthy of future research:

- the characteristics of the social support availiable to the patient;
- impulsiveness;
- reactions to provocation;
- ability to empathise;
- the nature of hallucinations and delusions.

Another important risk factor among the mentally disordered

may be substance abuse, and this subject is reviewed in Soyka (1994). The use of a weapon in past violence is also held by several authors to greatly increase risk of future *serious* violence (e.g. Dietz 1985).

The assessment of risk

Recently there has been a shift of emphasis away from 'dangerousness' and towards a broader concept of risk assessment. This move was summarised by Steadman *et al* (1993), drawing upon a recent report about violence from a public health perspective (US Department of Health and Human Services 1991) and a paper from the New York Academy of Medicine (1986):

- a move from a legal concept of dangerousness to a 'decision-making concept' of risk;
- that prediction should be considered as being on a continuum rather than a 'yes/no' dichotomy;
- that there should be a shift away from the notion that there can be a single prediction of risk, to a recognition that there is a continuing process of risk assessment that must be incorporated into the day-to-day management of mentally disordered people.

Carson (1991) edits the proceedings of a British multidisciplinary conference on risk-taking and mental health and stresses that in taking a risk there are chances of positive as well as negative consequences.

Despite this and the current limitations in predicting violence, dangerousness continues to be a major consideration of mental health professionals when deciding whether to detain or release the mentally disordered. The Department of Health has stressed the importance of considering the dangerousness of patients both in the new Code of Practice of the Mental Health Act (HMSO 1993), in a press release (DOH 1993a) about supervised discharge proposals (discussed in Crichton 1994) and within new supervision register proposals (DOH 1993b).

In the United States the implications of the *Tarasoff* case have fundamentally altered the clinicians' role in assessing violence and their responsibility to third parties (Beck 1985, 1987; Goldstein & Calderone 1992; Kaufman 1991; Leong *et al* 1992; Mackay 1990; and Poythress 1990).

The NHS Executive (1994) has published important guidelines on the discharge of mentally disordered people and their continuing care in the community which include a section on assessing potentially violent patients, included as Appendix A.

In individual cases a past history of violence is regarded as one of the best indicators of future violence. Taylor (1993) comments: 'The literature, indeed, repeats almost monotonously that the best predictor of future violence is past violence', and several studies have demonstrated this empirically (for example Aiken 1984; Convit *et al* 1988; Rofman *et al* 1980). Although past history of violence may be the best indicator of future violence, this in itself may not be very helpful if the risk of future violence is only modestly increased; for example Harry & Steadman (1988) found that a history of previous arrests would effectively predict only 5% of future offending.

These points do not make any easier the specific decision about whether and when to relax control and supervision of a mentally disordered offender who has a proven history of past violence, and this question is discussed in Chapters 5 and 6. In conclusion Prins (1990) suggests nine questions, in no order of priority, which may help in this decision, summarised in Table 2.

Table 2. Questions to ask when deciding whether to relax control over a mentally disordered offender with a history of violence (from Prins 1990)

1. Have past precipitants and stresses in the offender-patient's background been removed or sufficiently alleviated?
2. What is this offender-patient's current capacity for dealing with provocation ?
3. Have the clues to the offender-patient's self image been explored at sufficient depth?
4. How vulnerable and fragile does the offender-patient seem to be? Were the circumstances of the original offence the last straw in a series of stressful events, or does the individual see everybody else as hostile?
5. Was the behaviour person-specific or aimed at society in general?
6. Has the offender-patient come to terms, in part if not *in toto*, with the offending act?
7. Have the details about the original offence been examined?
8. Has the health care institution monitored the offender-patient's reaction to stress and temptation?
9. Has it been borne in mind that the offender-patient's denial of the original offence may reflect the truth?

References

AIKEN G.J.M. (1984) Assaults on staff in a locked ward: prediction and consequences. *Medicine, Science and the Law* **24** 199-207.

BECK J.C. (1985) Psychiatric assessment of potential violence: a reanalysis of the problem. In J.C. Beck (ed.) *The Potentially Violent Patient and the Tarasoff Decision in Psychiatric Practice*. Washington DC: American Psychiatric Press, pp. 83-9.

BECK J.C. (1987) The psychotherapist's duty to protect third parties from harm. *Mental and Physical Disability Law Reporter* **11** 141-8.

CARSON D. (1990) *Risk Taking in Mental Disorder*. Chichester: SLE Publications.

COCOZZA J. & STEADMAN H. (1976) The failure of psychiatric predictions of dangerousness: clear and convincing evidence. *Rutgers Law Review* **29** 1084-1111.

CONVIT A., JAEGER J. & LIN S. (1988) Predicting assaultiveness in psychiatric inpatients; a pilot study. *Hospital and Community Psychiatry* **39** 429-34.

CRICHTON J.H.M. (1994) Supervised discharge. *Medicine, Science and the Law.* **34** 319-20.

DOH (1993a) Press Release H93/908, 12 August 1993.

DOH (1993b) Press Release H93/1144, 28 December 1993.

DIETZ P.E. (1985) Hypothetical criteria for the prediction of individual criminality. In C.D. Webster, M.H. Ben-Aron & S.J. Hucker (eds) *Dangerousness: Probability and Prediction, Psychiatry and Public Policy* Cambridge: Cambridge University Press.

GOLDSTEIN R.L. & CALDERONE J.M. (1992) The Tarasoff raid: a new extension of the duty to protect. *Bulletin of the American Academy of Psychiatry and the Law* **20** 335-42.

HARRY B. & STEADMAN H. (1988) Arrest rates of patients treated at a community mental health centre. *Hospital and Community Psychiatry* **39** 862-6.

HMSO (1993) *The Mental Health Act 1983 Code of Practice* 2nd ed. London: HMSO.

KAUFMAN M. (1991) Post-Tarasoff legal developments and the mental health literature. *Bulletin of the Menninger Clinic* **55** 308-22.

LEONG G.B., ETH S. & SILVA J.A. (1992) The psychotherapist as witness for the prosecution: the criminalisation of Tarasoff. *American Journal of Psychiatry* **149** 1011-5.

LIDZ C.W., MULVEY E.P. & GARDENER W. (1993) The accuracy of predictions of violence to others. *Journal of the American Medical Association* **269** 1007-11.

LINK B., ANDREWS H. & CULLEN F. (1992) The violent and illegal behavior of mental patients reconsidered. *American Sociological Review* **57** 275-92.

LITWICK T.R., KIRSCHNER S.M. & WACK R.C. (1993) The assessment of dangerousness and predictions of violence: recent research and future prospects. *Psychiatric Quarterly* **64** 245-73.

MACKAY R.D. (1990) Dangerous patients. Third party safety and psychiatrist's duties – walking the Tarasoff tightrope. *Medicine, Science and the Law* **30** 52-6.

MONAHAN J. (1984) The prediction of violent behaviour: towards a second generation of theory and policy. *American Journal of Psychiatry* **141** 10-15.

MONAHAN J. (1988) Risk assessment of violence among the mentally disordered: generating useful knowledge. *International Journal of Law and Psychiatry* **11** 249-57.

MONAHAN J. (1993) Mental disorder and violence: another look. In S. Hodgins (ed.) *Mental Disorder and Crime.* Newbury Park, California: Sage Publications, pp. 294-5.

NHS EXECUTIVE (1994) *Guidance on the Discharge of Mentally Disordered People and their Continuing Care in the Community.* HSG (94)27. London: Department of Health.

3. The Prediction of Psychiatric Patient Violence

NEW YORK ACADEMY OF MEDICINE (1986) Homicide: the public health perspective. *Bulletin of the New York Academy of Medicine* **62** 373-624.

POYTHRESS N. (1990) Avoiding negligent release: contemporary clinical and risk management strategies. *American Journal of Psychiatry* **147** 994-7.

PRINS H. (1990) Social factors affecting the assessment of risk; with special reference to offender patients. In D. Carson (ed.). *Risk Taking in Mental Disorder*. Chichester: SLE Publications.

ROFMAN E.S., ASKINAZI C. & FANT E. (1980) The prediction of dangerous behaviour in emergency civil commitment. *American Journal of Psychiatry* **137** 1061-4.

SCOTT P.D. (1977) Assessing dangerousness in criminals. *British Journal of Psychiatry* **313** 127-42.

SOYKA M. (1994) Substance abuse and dependency as a risk factor for delinquency and violent behaviour in schizophrenic patients. *Journal of Clinical Forensic Medicine* **1** 3-7.

STEADMAN H.J., MONAHAN J., CLARK ROBBINS P., APPELBAUM P., GRISSO T., KLASSEN D., MULVEY E.P. & ROTH L. (1993) From dangerousness to risk assessment: implications for appropriate research strategies. In S. Hodgins (ed.) *Mental Disorder and Crime*. Newbury Park, California: Sage Publications.

SWANSON J., HOLZER C., GANJU V. & JONO R. (1990) Violence and psychiatric disorder in the community: evidence from the epidemiologic catchment area surveys. *Hospital and Community Psychiatry* **41** 761-70.

TAYLOR P.J. (1993) Mental illness and violence. In P.J. Taylor (ed.). *Violence in Society*. London: The Royal College of Physicians.

US DEPARTMENT OF HEALTH AND HUMAN SERVICES (1991) *Healthy People 2000: National Health Promotion and Disease Prevention Objectives*. Washington DC: Government Printing Office.

4

Risk Assessment and Management:
A Home Office Perspective

Jonathan Potts

Introduction

This chapter outlines some of the main factors which the Home Office, from its experience of dealing with restricted patient casework, has found to be particularly important in assessing and managing the risk of harm to the public posed by certain mentally disordered people who have been convicted of offences.

The Home Office role

The Home Secretary's responsibilities in relation to restricted patients were first introduced by the Mental Health Act (MHA) 1959. This gave effect to the recommendation of the Percy Royal Commission (1957) that mentally disordered offenders should be treated in hospitals rather than punished with imprisonment, but that if this were to be acceptable it should not, in the cases of more dangerous offenders, be left to the doctors and the hospital authorities alone to decide on significant moves towards liberty, including ultimately discharge into the community.

Restricted patients are those who have been made subject to a hospital order by the Crown Court where the court has decided that special restrictions are necessary 'for the protection of the public from serious harm' (S. 41(1) MHA 1983). They also include prisoners transferred to mental hospitals by warrant of the

Secretary of State (S.s 47-49 MHA 1983). The effect is that a restricted patient may not be

- given leave to go outside the hospital grounds;
- transferred to another hospital under different management;
- discharged from hospital;

without the Home Secretary's consent.

Since the coming into force of the Mental Health Act 1983, a Mental Health Review Tribunal has had power to order the conditional or absolute discharge of a restricted patient. The tribunal must have regard to considerations of public safety, and will take into account any observations of the Secretary of State, who may be represented before it.

In considering proposals relating to restricted patients the Home Office needs to satisfy itself that any risk to the public has been properly identified and evaluated, and that sound measures have been taken to guard against it. Home Office officials are not clinicians and do not pretend to make clinical judgments. The Home Office in this context is looking at risk in the broader sense that judges on the Parole Board do. The task is to undertake a detached and rigorous scrutiny of the proposal made by the Responsible Medical Officer (the psychiatrist in charge of a case as designated in the MHA), to see how far it appears complete, soundly argued, balanced and objective.

The collective experience available to the Home Office in carrying out this task embraces a view of all the cases of restricted patients, of whom there are upward of 3,600, including some 1,500 in the community on conditional discharge. Officials are acquainted with the hospitals where such patients are detained, and with the medical and other staff there. We keep in close touch with cases and do not confine our interest to the moment when a decision has to be taken.

The concept of risk

Naturally it is not possible literally to 'predict' whether someone is going to do harm in a given situation, although in the short term certain warning signs – changes in mood or behaviour – may indicate that a particular person is more likely to do something violent or destructive. In looking at the longer-term protection of the public we are concerned with the following:

- *assessment of risk*: not just 'how likely' it is that a person will do harm, but *in what circumstances* the risk of harm arises;
- *management of risk*: how the risky circumstances can be avoided, or the patient brought to understand and deal effectively with those circumstances; and, if things do start to go wrong, is there a clear, sound procedure for picking up the signs and taking appropriate action?

In assessing the proposals made to us by hospitals for the transfer or discharge of restricted patients, we look for evidence both of accurate assessment and of effective risk management. The latter will usually involve both work done already with the patient in preparation for the next move to more challenging conditions (this may take many years), and a package of prospective measures to help the patient meet the challenge successfully.

If the proposed move is appropriate, justified and safe, the Secretary of State will give his consent to it.

What to look for?

The remainder of this chapter outlines some of the factors which we consider important in assessing and managing risk. The Home Office supplies Responsible Medical Officers with a checklist of matters which we expect to be addressed in their reports and recommendations; this is included as Appendix B.

First some general refections. Risk is not something that can be 'diagnosed' in the patient. It involves looking at a complex combination of things, in particular:

- the patient's current mental state, behaviour and outlook;
- full family, personal, psychiatric, ordinary medical and offending histories;
- an understanding of what triggers violence or other problem behaviour in that particular patient;
- other things going on that are relevant to the patient, such as quality of support from family and friends outside, and any changes in this;
- the situation of any past or known potential victims and the patient's attitude towards them and theirs towards him or her;
- the situation into which it is proposed the patient will move, looked at dynamically – in other words not just as things are now but taking into account all the main foreseeable contingencies.

The factors found in good risk assessments

More specifically, what are the factors we look for, and which we expect to find in good risk assessments? These can be summarised under the following headings:

- quality and range of information
- completeness and objectivity of analysis
- concrete evidence of progress
- realistic forward planning

Quality and range of information

We expect a good risk assessment to:

- show that *all* risk factors have been considered even where some turn out to be inapplicable: at least then the issue has been thought about, not just forgotten;
- draw on the observations of *a range of care staff* and give suitable weight to other perspectives than that of the psychiatrist: observations of the patient's interaction with other patients and with (for example) nursing staff can be particularly valuable;
- give due weight to past as well as current information: with long stay patients, doctors may change, and in any case the recent past may assume a disproportionate significance;
- in particular, an understanding of the *index offence*, the offence which led to the imposition of a hospital order with restrictions (or to a prison sentence followed by transfer to hospital under a restriction direction), and of any events since of comparable significance, is crucial. What motivated the patient to violence, and what triggered it?
- is there agreement about diagnosis; if not, what has been done to clarify it? Are any remaining disagreements about diagnosis significant to the understanding of the index offence?
- is there sufficient information about the patient's family and other important relationships, and the patient's relationship with past or known potential victims?

Completeness and objectivity of analysis

- does the analysis focus on evidence, not just opinion?
- is it clear where 'information' has come from? If there is any *prima facie* doubt about it, has it been corroborated or verified? Has the observation come from someone competent to make it? Has the patient fed a line to carers?
- is a patient's reported 'insight' real, or is there any indication that what the patient says about himself or herself has been 'learned', for example from therapy?
- multidisciplinary joint assessments are valuable, but they can also result in 'compromise' conclusions which belie

important differences of view and important anxieties on the part of some staff; it is essential therefore that divergencies of view are distinguished, not fudged.

Concrete evidence of progress

The following issues are important:

- have the issues around the *index offence* been addressed positively, and how far have they been resolved?
- what is the concrete evidence of change, beyond 'good behaviour'?
- evidence of the patient's motivation to change and to progress.
- what has medication achieved? Is the patient compliant? Is he or she likely to remain so in more challenging circumstances? Are there particular factors which affect compliance?

Realistic forward planning

Restricted patients will usually spend many years in hospital and further years under medical and social supervision upon their discharge into the community. There are likely to be a number of key stages on the way to successful rehabilitation, each of which will be crucial to the longer-term outcome as well as significant in its own right. Just as there is a need to keep past events, especially the index offence and any analogous incidents firmly in mind at each stage, so it is also important to have a clear and realistic view of what is to be achieved at the next stage and future stages after that.

Good planning and good risk management will involve the following, as key changes in the patient's treatment and care are first planned and then executed:

- gradual testing of the patient in new conditions, which can be accomplished by gradually increasing leave freedoms

and by longer periods of trial leave at the prospective new hospital or community accommodation – providing patient, carers and public with the safety net of return to the old institution if things do not work out;
- a full appreciation of the stresses and challenges which the patient will face and of his or her ability to cope with these;
- an effective care plan;
- concrete, tested measures to anticipate and deal with any problem areas such as drinking or stressful relationships (including an understanding on the part of the patient of these factors and how to deal with them);
- early warning systems with provision for clear, rapid action if things start to go wrong;
- a good flow of information between care team members and respect for one another;
- continuity between old and new care teams, preferably with overlap and full sharing of information, and an understanding of its significance;
- the flexibility to be able to change course and abandon plans completely if the patient's condition or outlook changes or new information comes to light.

Some observed weaknesses in risk assessment

It should be stressed that most proposals that come to the Home Office from Responsible Medical Officers are of good quality – aided, we hope, by constructive interaction with the Department. But it may be useful, briefly, to enumerate the deficiencies that can sometimes be found. Many of these are, of course, the reverse of the good features mentioned above.

In no particular order, the following are traps to be avoided:

- events or issues may be minimised because they happened long ago – the 'model' patient who in fact has not been challenged;
- over-reliance on recent progress after many uneventful years;

41

- a sudden change of view on the part of the care team, possibly influenced by extraneous considerations;
- other extraneous factors, not openly recognised as must be proper and necessary, but permitted insidiously to affect the assessment of risk;
- infrequency or discontinuity of assessment and reporting;
- not verifying what the patient or others say;
- apparently believing what the patient or others say in spite of clear contrary evidence;
- the manipulative patient, driving a wedge between carers or 'charming' them;
- superficial acceptance of learned 'insight' and 'remorse';
- lack of openness between carers or between them and others concerned in the arrangements;
- discounting information which does not support the hoped-for outcome;
- the need to be decisive/successful;
- being too close to the patient/not wanting confrontation.

Reference

PERCY (Chairman) (1957). *Report on Law relating to Mental Illness and Mental Deficiency 1954-1957*. Royal Commission Cmnd 169. London: HMSO.

Risk Assessment and Management in Clinical Context

Adrian Grounds

This chapter focuses on risk assessment and decision-making in psychiatric work with individual patients. My theme is that individual risk assessment must be grounded in history. This is a frequently repeated message, but I want to examine in some detail what it means.

Before I do so the topic needs to be put in context: first, of the current structure of psychiatric services, and secondly, of the state of current research knowledge.

Contemporary psychiatric services and public protection

The structure of general psychiatric services has changed so radically in the last forty years that a major reappraisal is needed of what contemporary services can realistically deliver in terms of containment and public protection. In essence, psychiatric services are not equipped in the way they used to be to protect society from crimes committed by the mentally disordered.

Paul Bowden (1993) has cogently argued that the important change has not been the closure of hospital beds, but the change in the ethos of psychiatric care that preceded it. He wrote:

> it was not the decline of the mental hospital that led to the translocation of large numbers of chronic psychotics into the community, it was their opening in the first place (p. 82).

He quotes from Henry Rollin's (1969) description of this change in Horton Hospital.

> In 1938 the 'escapes' of male patients from Horton ... recorded in meticulous detail ... numbered exactly eight, ... security in those days was one of the hallmarks of an efficient hospital and, judged by this criterion, Horton must have been highly regarded.
>
> ... with a great sense of urgency ward doors were unlocked and locks removed from windows ... the hideous railings which fenced in the airing courts ... were at last torn down ... as freedom came in through the open doors, security went out through the windows (p. 103).

Similarly, David Clarke (1993), described Fulbourn Hospital when he arrived as a young Medical Superintendent in 1953 as follows:

> You were taken in by somebody with a key who unlocked the door and then locked it behind you. The crashing of keys in the locks was an essential part of asylum life then, just as it is today in jails (p. 78).
>
> ... Then there were the airing courts. Grey, big courts paved with tarmac, surrounded by a wall twelve feet high and a hundred men milling round ... A couple of bored young male nurses standing on 'point duty', looking at them, ready to hit anyone who got out of line ... (p. 79).
>
> There was a pattern to the day. The patients were turned out to the airing court, counted out and counted in. Then they sat at their tables for their meals; spoons and forks handed out and the food put on the table ... Then the spoons and forks were all taken in and washed by the staff and counted. Nobody left the table until all the cutlery was counted (pp. 79-80).
>
> The job of the nurses was to watch the patients to see that they didn't escape or harm one another (p. 80).
>
> If a certified patient escaped and broke into a house and stole, the only person the aggrieved householder could sue was the medical superintendent. So within the hospital he had absolute power ... for instance, when he saw a nurse hand a key to a patient, and fired him on the spot (p. 81).
>
> ... the easier thing for the doctor in charge is to say, 'Don't let that patient out.' It's more difficult to say, 'Let him out rather more often.' When they say, 'What'll happen if he hits someone?' you have to say, 'I'll answer for that!'

I came to see in later years that my job had been to give people a feeling of security ... a belief that if they took risks, they wouldn't be abandoned to a Committee of Enquiry.
... That was the first phase, opening the doors (p. 83).

The path of progress entailed overturning the primary emphasis on security. Today, the last vestiges of the old regimes remain only in the special hospitals. It is this that has led to such harsh criticism of them, because such regimes are seen as having no justification now.

The Boynton report (DHSS 1980) on Rampton Hospital in 1980 noted:

The hospital appears to have been in a backwater and the main currents of thought about the care of mental patients have passed it by (p. iii).

The Health Advisory Service report (NHS Health Advisory Service, DHSS Social Services Inspectorate 1988) on Broadmoor Hospital in 1988 described:

... regimes which are outdated and excessively custodial and depersonalising (para 59).

The Ashworth Inquiry of 1992 (DOH 1992a) spoke of 'the culture of denigration and devaluing of patients' (p. 148); the hospital's 'outmoded style of care' (p. 164); and of how '... Ashworth and its problems belonged to a past era' (p. 164).

There is no reason any longer for an attitude that permits any derogation from the precepts of therapy; no lingering attachment to the unwholesome image of the criminal lunatic asylum; and no reflection of the punitive aspects of the contemporary penal system (p. 253).

The struggle to assert the primacy of therapy rather than security is what the special hospital service is grappling with now, in the same way as was done in the local hospitals by medical superintendents and others in the post-war decades. We

45

have inherited their achievements, but what have these changes meant for public protection?

The contemporary pattern of local psychiatric services – with fewer beds, shorter admissions and care being provided outside hospital – results in patients spending longer periods of time at risk of committing offences in the community. The challenge for community psychiatric care has been to work out how to provide the multiple functions of the hospital outside an institutional framework. Providing the functional equivalents of housing, occupation, social networks and medical treatment has been on the whole a story of progress. However, providing the functional equivalent of public protection, control and containment is an unsolved challenge.

It is not surprising that the last generation of critical inquiries into scandals in mental hospitals, revealing cruel, dehumanising aspects of custodial care (Martin 1984), has given way to inquiries into scandals of community psychiatry, revealing failures to provide custody, public protection and continuity of care (e.g. the Report of the Clunis Inquiry, Ritchie 1994). In Nicholas Rose's words:

> Yesterday's 'scandals' of the institution have already been replaced by today's 'scandals' of the community (Rose 1986, p. 206).

It is also not surprising that there has been the recent political response of introducing new guidelines on the discharge of mentally disordered people from hospital (NHS Executive 1994a; see extract below in Appendix A), and proposals for supervision registers (NHS Executive 1994b).

Within this tension between, on the one hand, progressive services seeking to maximise autonomy of patients and provide care in the least restrictive setting, and, on the other hand, the worries about and demands for safety and public protection, attention has become focused on risk assessment. Here is the means of rescue: the procedure which is expected to steer a safe course between these opposing demands so that we will correctly identify and contain the dangerous patients but not the others.

It has to be recognised at the outset, first that there are limits

46

to our knowledge about risk, secondly that there are limits to our ability to assess it, and thirdly that there are limits imposed upon us by the structure and ethos of our services. In future years we may make progress in the first two. As far as the third is concerned, we cannot put the clock back. We cannot expect our present pattern of services to deliver public protection as powerfully as the edifice of custodial, secure confinement that was overturned a generation ago. The incarceration of the mentally disordered is a powerful means of incapacitating them, in the sense of preventing crime. However, in community-based services, with minimum use of compulsory powers and a small secure unit estate, the addition of risk assessment, assertive follow-up and closer supervision can not be expected to provide an equivalent level of social defence against harmful acts by people with mental disorder.

It is officially recognised that these new measures are not a panacea and not every disaster can be predicted and prevented (see below, Appendix A). However, that recognition is ultimately of little comfort to practitioners when a disaster occurs, and it does not protect them from a public inquiry (NHS Executive 1994a, para 34). Nor should it, from the point of view of victims and the wider public. In dealing with issues of risk, contemporary psychiatric services carry a heavy burden.

There is another pressure that impinges on risk assessment, namely the limited availability of secure hospital beds for patients that need them. There is a widespread recognition that current numbers of secure unit places are inadequate (DOH 1992b), and in recent months there has been a crisis since all available provision is full. Last week one of my colleagues was an hour behind in his clinic, telephoning fruitlessly to find a secure bed for one of his patients. We have seriously ill and assaultive patients remanded in custody and being precariously managed in local hospitals who cannot be found secure beds. At the same time our purchasing commission is telling us that if it is to provide more funding to supervise high-risk patients in the community there will have to be reductions in the use of regional secure unit beds because it cannot afford both. These are the hard realities that impinge on the decision-making we are discussing, and they set structural limits to what can be achieved.

Research on risk and mental disorder

Individual assessment also needs to be carried out with awareness of relevant research knowledge. This is of two kinds. First, there is a literature on the nature of risk assessment and decision-making (see, for example, Monahan 1988; Pollock *et al* 1989). This provides a framework for thinking about what we are doing. Secondly, there is the literature on risk and mental disorder. This tells us what we can know, principally about offending risk in populations rather than individuals.

Theoretical and conceptual issues

Some key points to emphasise from the theoretical and conceptual literature are as follows. First, the assessment of risk involves consideration of three different components, namely an outcome (e.g. an offence), the likelihood of the outcome, and a time frame (Carson 1993). Secondly, predictions of the future can be wrong in two ways: there are false positive outcomes – harm occurs when it was predicted it would not; and false negative outcomes: harm does not occur when it was predicted that it would (Monahan 1988). In decisions about release or detention of patients both errors can have adverse consequences. Thirdly, in clinical assessment there is the danger of hindsight bias (Pollock *et al* 1989). In the context of a public inquiry, this is an important point. When looking back at the history of someone who has committed a serious offence, we focus selectively on the factors that appear to have contributed to the outcome. This can make an event that is statistically unlikely – an offence with a low base rate – look highly probable or even inevitable. This in turn can lead us to overestimate future dangerousness (Fischoff 1975, quoted in Pollock *et al*

1989). Fourthly, clinical assessment is not primarily about making an accurate prediction but about making informed, defensible decisions about dangerous behaviour. The test is not one of accuracy, but how defensible the decision is in terms of social realities and current scientific knowledge (Pollock *et al* 1989).

Clinical and epidemiological research

Some of the key messages from current research knowledge are as follows.

Actuarial studies – i.e. statistical studies of risk in large populations – suggest that factors predictive of violent behaviour in the general population include past crime, particularly violence, young age, being male and a history of alcohol or opiate abuse (Monahan 1981). A recent review of research on re-offending by mentally disordered offenders (Murray 1989) suggests that correlates of reconviction among mentally disordered offenders include the same factors.

Longitudinal prospective birth cohort studies suggest that people with psychoses are at greater risk of criminal offending, particularly violent offending. The risk is further increased if the history of psychosis is associated with an additional history of substance abuse in childhood (Hodgins 1992; 1993).

It is likely that active symptoms of severe mental illness also increase risk of violence. Two recent major studies (Swanson *et al* 1990; Link *et al* 1992) indicate that people *actively* experiencing serious psychotic symptoms (e.g. delusions and hallucinations) 'are involved in violent behaviour at rates several times those of non-disordered members of the general population, and that this difference persists even when a wide array of demographic and social factors are taken into consideration' (Monahan 1993, p. 295). Taylor's (1985) retrospective study of men with psychotic illnesses who had committed crimes of violence found that the offences tended to have occurred in direct response to active psychotic symptoms, especially delusions.

However, this increased risk should be kept in perspective. It does not imply that the mentally disordered as a whole pose a significant social threat. The great majority (approximately 90%) of people who are actively mentally ill in the community are not violent (Monahan 1993).

Clinical risk assessment

Large-scale statistical studies such as those cited above are only of limited help in assessing risk in an individual case. A further set of questions should be asked in considering the possible future behaviour of a particular individual. As a practical guide, Monahan (1981) produced a useful research-based checklist of questions to be addressed by clinicians in predicting risk of violent behaviour in a particular case. Key questions include those listed in the Table 3 below.

These questions provide a bench mark against which opinions about risk might be tested. Are all these questions addressed? Are the answers to them well substantiated?

Table 3. Questions for the clinician in predicting violent behaviour (from Monahan 1981)

1. What are the person's relevant demographic characteristics?
2. What is the person's history of violent behaviour?
3. What is the base rate of violent behaviour among individuals of this person's background?
4. What are the sources of stress in the person's current environment?
5. What cognitive and emotional factors indicate that the person may be predisposed to cope with stress in a violent manner?
6. What cognitive and emotional factors indicate that the person may be predisposed to cope with stress in a non-violent manner?
7. How similar are the contexts in which the person has used violent coping mechanisms in the past to the contexts in which the person is likely to function in the future?
8. In particular, who are the likely victims of the person's violent behaviour, and how available are they?
9. What means does the person possess to commit violence?

Assessing the individual history

The assessment of the individual must be grounded in history. The aim in looking back is to discover and understand patterns of behaviour, and to elucidate their context. Then, in looking forward, to look for evidence of repetition of context and to specify the situations in which harm is most likely to occur. Conclusions should be expressed in cautious, conditional terms, making clear the level of confidence in which the opinion can be held (Pollock *et al* 1989). What follows is a selection of practical points about the assessment of history; this is not a comprehensive account.

History is established from records, informants and interview. It can be very time-consuming. The idea that thorough risk assessment can be introduced without resource implications because it is only a matter of formalising existing good practice is a nonsense which takes no account of the reality of the pressures on our services. A consultant colleague described to me last week how on his acute ward, where there are patients sleeping in the corridor, there may be only five minutes to make discharge decisions and not enough time to bring patients in to ward meetings to talk to them. And this is in Cambridge, not Inner London.

Records

Records must be examined in detail when establishing histories of violent behaviour. In clinical records, nursing notes are often more accurate and detailed than medical notes in this regard. When criminal offences have been committed in the past, the criminal record listing convictions, dates and sentences gives a useful, although not always accurate, indication of gravity of offences and how seriously they were regarded by the courts. One might not lose sleep over convictions for Common Assault, but if it is GBH or Wounding, significant injury may have been inflicted and the details must be ascertained. Where very grave offences have been committed in the past, the police account or key prosecution statements are a vital benchmark, and should form part of the current clinical record of any patient under treatment or supervision. The absence of such material can make risk assessment practically impossible.

In making judgements about past violent behaviour, not only the actual harm done but the potential for serious harm should be assessed. In seeing local inpatients referred for transfer to the regional secure unit, violence involving weapons or attempts at strangling may not have caused much actual harm because of quick intervention, but it may have been potentially life-threatening in a way that violent outbursts with kicking and use of fists are not, although the latter may have caused more distress.

Fear and alarm are not reliable criteria of risk. There is too much fear and worry about some patients and too little about others. Some time ago I saw a patient on an acute ward who had recently been stopped from running down the ward with a kitchen knife. The staff were not unduly concerned because he had been intercepted without incident almost immediately. However, it emerged from interviewing this man, who had a paranoid illness and severe sexual difficulties, that he had an erotic fixation and homicidal thoughts which he found difficult to control towards a specific doctor. On seeing her in the ward he had felt overwhelmed by vengeance, went to the kitchen to get the knife and ran down the corridor determined to kill her. He had behaved similarly in the past, although again without harm resulting. The ward staff were surprised at the decision that he should go to the regional secure unit. They were much more used to patients who actually assaulted them being turned down because they were not thought dangerous enough.

Interview

This case emphasises the importance of the interview. The interview has multiple purposes; to establish history and psychiatric diagnosis in the usual way, but also to gain an understanding of the patient's biography and offending from the inside. The world has to be viewed through the patient's eyes. The personal history, the offending and its context have to be understood in this way as well as in terms of external factors and independent reports. In the case of people with psychotic symptoms, particular attention must be paid to the detailed content and the intensity of the abnormal beliefs and experiences. How 'driven' is the patient by them? (Taylor 1985). To what extent have they been acted on and have any plans been thought about? What holds the patient back and stops him or her acting on the symptoms?

There are two other second-order purposes of the interview: to assess the patient's insight into his (or her) behaviour, and to assess the kind of relationship that can be established with him – in terms of cooperation, therapeutic alliance, supervisability, and the potential transference and counter-transference phenomena.

The review of the history should establish a detailed record of past events, an understanding of the relation between the offending and the psychiatric disorder, and the situational context of the offending. It should also if possible give a sense of how the patient has experienced events: how the world was and is to him. Particularly for the non-psychotic offender, history-taking includes this psychodynamic aspect, listening for the links between past and present as the story is told. Sometimes the same words are used without the patient realising it. The resonance of the offence setting with past experience can make understandable what at first sight was inexplicable (Scott 1977). As Peter Scott put it so simply:

> The impact of a breaking marriage may be very different on a man whose mother deserted when he was five (p. 130).

Scott's paper 'Assessing dangerousness in criminals', published in 1977 in the *British Journal of Psychiatry*, remains full of measured, clinical wisdom on the topic of clinical assessment.

There is no substitute for seeking a thorough understanding of the patient's experience in making proper judgements. An example is evaluating lack of remorse. To say a patient has no remorse conveys no useful information on its own. On the one hand, lack of remorse may mean that the patient believes his or her action was justified – for example, to avenge some wrongdoing. If so, the implications for assessing future risk will depend on whether the reaction was proportionate or disproportionate; whether the patient's beliefs about the wrongdoing were true, untrue or psychotic; and whether he or she has a sense of relief and completion, or a sense of persisting revenge and unfinished business. On the other hand, however, absence of remorse may mean something quite different. It could indicate a more widespread lack of capacity for empathy. To make well-founded judgements the psychological understanding has to be thorough and specific.

Looking forward

The purpose of the history is to identify the possible situations of risk in the future. Assessing the likelihood of their occurrence may be more difficult. Sometimes it may only be possible to outline a situation of risk in general terms. For example, in a condition such as morbid jealousy, one may be able to be very specific and say that future risk is of violence towards future longstanding heterosexual partners, and that there is no significant risk outside this situation. But in another case of a patient with chronic schizophrenia, the history may include a wide variety of offending and violence when the patient is actively psychotic and not taking medication. For this person it may only be possible to specify a general situation of risk, namely being unmedicated, and no well-based judgements can be made beyond that about what might happen, to whom, and how serious the harm might be.

Distinguishing between worry and risk

Risk needs to be distinguished from worry. They are not well correlated, and judgements and decisions based on worry may not be well founded. The problem is that feelings of worry are expressed by professionals in the vocabulary of risk. The feeling 'I am very worried about X' is likely to be translated into 'X is a high risk' in written and spoken communications. Worry may, however, be excessive or insufficient in relation to the risk. The test is the same as for risk: how well grounded is it in history?

Management of risk

Identifying possible situations of risk enables preventive measures to be considered. There are two aspects: first, current measures in response to perceived risk; secondly, longer-term monitoring and supervision.

Current measures

When a current risk is perceived, the measures taken should be specific and proportionate, and should bear a rational relationship to the risk and the anticipated harm. Often measures taken are not like this, particularly in the aftermath of a violent incident or when worry is high. There are many examples in psychiatric practice and in the field of child protection, e.g. in the use of 'specialling' of patients and supervised access visits to children. Overreaction can have adverse effects. Unnecessary measures which are experienced by patients as oppressive may undermine their cooperation, put pressure on them and reduce openness. Again it is history that should be the guide in order to avoid the alternative dangers of over- and under-reaction.

An example of an irrational response occurred after the escape of Alan Reeve from Broadmoor some years ago, when one of the measures taken was the confiscation of binoculars from all patients who had them – for watching wildlife from their windows, etc. Presumably the concern was that they might survey the perimeter wall, over which Alan Reeve had climbed, to plan a similar escape. In fact the skill that enabled Alan Reeve to escape was exceptional athletic ability. Perhaps this should have been targeted instead!

Patients who have been violent are vulnerable to poor clinical judgement and poor discharge planning. Fear and dislike may colour decisions about them; there may be signals of rejection; precipitate discharge; imposition of 'contracts' of good behaviour which they are unlikely to keep; and patients with chronic psychotic disorders can be given revised diagnoses of personality disorder. We should be deeply suspicious of this practice. People do not develop primary personality disorders in their middle decades. The revised diagnosis may be used to justify exclusion from further psychiatric care, and to justify spurious attributions of 'responsibility' onto the patient, when really this is a process of clinical staff disowning their responsibility to the patient.

Measures in response to perceived risk also have to take account of public expectations and those of the criminal justice system.

A case illustrating these problems concerns a man with a psychotic illness who absconded from hospital, stole £40 from a nurse's handbag before he went, and later set a fire in a famous city centre church under the influence of voices. He should receive a hospital order. However, the nurses do not want him back because of the theft and are suggesting that he is not ill; the consultant accepts that he is ill but does not want him back if he is put on a restriction order, which no doubt the Court may wish to impose.

Monitoring and supervision

Longer-term responses to risk are monitoring and supervision. Supervision is not primarily a surveillance and crime control process, but a framework of support. Monitoring depends centrally on the maintenance of a relationship with the patient, with every effort being made to achieve cooperation, openness and trust. Surveillance that is onerous and outside a framework of support may reduce the cooperation and disclosure on which effective continuing risk assessment depends. Susanne Dell and I have recently completed some research funded by the Home Office on the supervision of conditionally discharged restricted patients. I am not yet able to disclose the results of what was a fascinating study, but suffice it to say that the overwhelming impression was of how positively the supervision process was regarded by all concerned as a means of enabling support and continuation of care.

Assessing supervisability is a matter of judging the patient's likely cooperation, capacity for honest reporting, and the possibility of a working relationship of mutual trust.

Supervision may involve a long-term commitment, and as time passes the history must never be forgotten. The details, the original account, should remain fixed in the records because they may not remain fixed in our memories. When I first went to work in Broadmoor twelve years ago one of the induction procedures for new staff was to visit the 'museum'. Here in glass cases were objects such as the stone used in the nineteenth century to hit a medical superintendent over the head in the chapel; and Mawdsley's teaspoon, with its sharpened handle (I will spare you the details of what he did with it). The museum visit was not only an old-fashioned initiation ceremony worthy of Goffman's 'Asylums', but a reminder of the importance of the particular, an image of how we have to remember what has happened in our patients' lives.

I would like to make one final point about long-term supervision, which returns to the opening theme about the contemporary context of psychiatric services. Long-term supervision does not fit easily with two of the core principles that increasingly govern purchasing in the Health Service. First, that purchasing by Health Authorities should be of health rather than social care; secondly, that purchasing should focus on the delivery of health gain. In the long-term supervision of patients, health and social care may be impossible to separate and the health component may be small. Secondly, the aim of supervision is not to deliver health gain in the sense of short- or medium-term psychological change. That is not a realistic goal. The aim is to maintain long-term stability. What are our outcome measures? Good outcomes are silent, the absence of disaster. But disaster can not always be prevented.

References

BOWDEN P. (1993) New directions for service provision: a personal view. In W. Watson and A.T. Grounds (eds) *The Mentally Disordered Offender in an Era of Community Care: New Directions in Provision.* Cambridge: Cambridge University Press, pp. 78-85.

CARSON D. (1993) *Risk Taking: Developing Analyses, Procedures, Policies and Strategies in Health and Social Work.* (Workshop papers). University of Southampton, Faculty of Law.

CLARKE D.H. (1993) Interview with Brian Barraclough (1985) In G. Wilkinson (ed.) *Talking About Psychiatry.* London: Gaskell, pp. 73-97.

DOH (1992a) *Report of the Committee of Inquiry into Complaints about Ashworth Hospital.* Cm 2028-I. London: HMSO.

DOH (1992b) *Review of Health and Social Services for Mentally Disordered Offenders and Others Requiring Similar Services: Final Summary Report.* Cmd 2088. London: HMSO.

DHSS (1980) *Report of the Review of Rampton Hospital.* Cmnd 8073. London: HMSO.

FISCHOFF B. (1975) Hindsight = Foresight: The effect of outcome knowledge on judgement under uncertainty. *Journal of Experimental Psychology: Human Perception and Performance.* 1 288-99.

HODGINS S. (1992) Mental disorder, intellectual deficiency and crime: evidence from a birth cohort. *Archives of General Psychiatry.* 49 476-83.

HODGINS S. (1993) The criminality of mentally disordered persons. In S. Hodgins (ed.) *Mental Disorder and Crime.* London: Sage, pp. 3-21.

LINK B., ANDREWS H., & CULLEN F. (1992) The violent and illegal behaviour of mental patients reconsidered. *American Sociological Review.* 57 275-92.

MARTIN J.P. (1984) *Hospitals in Trouble.* Oxford: Blackwell.

MONAHAN J. (1981) *The Clinical Prediction of Violent Behaviour.* Maryland: US Department of Health and Human Services.

MONAHAN J. (1988) Risk assessment of violence among the mentally disordered: generating useful knowledge. *International Journal of Law and Psychiatry.* 11 249-57.

MONAHAN J. (1993) Mental disorder and violence: another look. In S. Hodgins (ed.) *Mental Disorder and Crime.* Newbury Park, Ca.: Sage, pp. 287-302.

MURRAY D.J. (1989) *Review of Research on Reoffending of Mentally Disordered Offenders.* (Research and Planning Unit Paper 55). London: Home Office.

NHS EXECUTIVE (1994) *Guidance on the Discharge of Mentally Disor-*

dered *People and their Continuing Care in the Community.* HSG(94)27. London: Department of Health.

NHS EXECUTIVE (1994b) *Introduction of Supervision Registers for Mentally Ill People from 1 April 1994.* HSG(94)5. London: DOH.

NHS HEALTH ADVISORY SERVICE, DHSS SOCIAL SERVICES INSPECTORATE (1988) *Report on Services provided by Broadmoor Hospital.* HAS/SSI(88)SH-1. London: DHSS.

POLLOCK N., McBAIN I. & WEBSTER C.D. (1989) Clinical decision making and the assessment of dangerousness. In K. Howells and C.R. Hollin (eds) *Clinical Approaches to Violence.* Oxford: John Wiley.

RITCHIE J.H. (Chairman) (1994) *The Report of the Inquiry into the Care and Treatment of Christopher Clunis.* London: HMSO.

ROLLIN H. (1969) *The Mentally Abnormal Offender and the Law.* Oxford: Pergamon Press.

ROSE N. (1986) Law, rights and psychiatry. In P. Miller and N. Rose (eds) *The Power of Psychiatry.* Cambridge: Polity Press.

SCOTT P.D. (1977) Assessing dangerousness in criminals. *British Journal of Psychiatry.* **131** 127-42.

SWANSON J., HOLZER C., GANJU V. & JONO R. (1990) Violence and psychiatric disorder in the community: evidence from the epidemiologic catchment area surveys. *Hospital and Community Psychiatry.* **41** 761-70.

TAYLOR P.J. (1985) Motives for offending among violent and psychotic men. *British Journal of Psychiatry.* **147** 491-8.

PART III

The Response to
Psychiatric Patient Violence

6

The Response to Psychiatric Inpatient Violence

John Crichton

Introduction

Like any institution, a psychiatric ward depends on rules and order to function. Serious patient violence may be rare, but minor acts of violence and other misdemeanours, such as swearing at staff and refusal to keep minor rules, are an everyday part of psychiatric ward life. Psychiatric professionals have a particular challenge in that those they care for may not follow the rules of normal social behaviour and some may be unwilling patients. One function of psychiatric professionals is not only to care for their patients but also to manage disturbed or disruptive behaviour. The Code of Practice of the Mental Health Act (1983) gives advice on the management of patients presenting particular management problems (HMSO 1993), mainly concentrating on general preventive measures and the immediate management of dangerous situations rather than medium- or long-term management. The medium- and long-term management of disruptive behaviour is crucial to the success of the discharge of a patient and his or her care in the community, and raises many, often controversial, issues, some of which are discussed in this chapter.

Psychiatric control has had its critics and sometimes rests uneasily with dedicated staff who do not readily wish to use restrictive powers (Tantum 1991). Szasz (1961), for example, has been included as a leading member of the 'Anti-psychiatry

School', although he specifically denies he is anti-psychiatry. Szasz argues against any compulsory hospital detention and suggests that any criminal acts caused by a mentally disordered offender should be dealt with in the same way as those of any other offender in the courts. Clare (1976) and Wing (1978) defend psychiatry against such critics, but there is recent concern that some anti-psychiatry views are regaining popularity (Marks 1994).

Psychiatric control requires a balance between the respect for an individual's self-determination and the consideration of safety within the hospital and in the community.

A historical perspective

Psychiatric control has a long history; there is evidence of restrictive powers over the mentally disordered in the time of Plato (Sauders 1970) and in ancient Rome (Walker 1968). Before the move to the great Victorian asylums the control was often that of iron shackles, strait-waistcoats and the locked door of the 'mad-house' (Parry-Jones 1972; Porter 1987). Not all of the 'mad-houses' were as grim as later Victorian reformers were to suggest, but there was a reliance on mechanical restraint:

> Restraining the anger and violence of madmen is always necessary for preventing their hurting themselves or others; but this restraint is always to be considered as a remedy. Angry passions are always rendered more violent by the indulgence of the impetuous motions they produce; and which their passions would otherwise occasion. Restraint therefore is useful and ought to be complete (Cullen 1780).

Moral management searched for a more humane way to treat the mentally disordered and rested primarily on argument and persuasion. Ultimately, however, moral treatment also used physical restraint if other methods failed. The Reverend Willis, for example, in his management of George III, was frequently reported as telling the King to calm down or be placed in a strait-waistcoat (MacAlpine & Hunter 1969). William Tuke set

64

up the York Retreat as a model asylum which embraced moral therapy, but there was still coercion to engender self control:

> Lunatics quickly perceive, or if not, they are informed on the first occasion, that their treatment depends in great measure, upon their conduct. Coercion thus flowing as a sort of necessary consequence, and being executed in a manner which marks the reluctance of the attendant, it seldom exacerbates the violent patient, or produces that feverish and sometimes furious irritability, in which the maniacal character is completely developed: and which all power of self control is developed (Tuke 1813).

Public anxiety and concern over conditions in private madhouses grew, leading to a number of parliamentary inquiries at the beginning of the nineteenth century. One such inquiry heard in 1815 about William Norris, a 55-year-old Bedlam patient kept in a rigid metal harness for fourteen years (Porter 1987). Eventually these inquiries led the building of the great Victorian county asylums and the creation of the Lunacy Commission in 1845 (Jones 1993). The Commission in its annual reports gave details of psychiatric abuses, including in its eighth report (1851) the case of a patient who bit the arm of the proprietor of Dunston Lodge, Co. Durham, Mr J.E. Wilkinson. Subsequently the patient was placed in a strait-jacket, flogged and secluded. Later his two front teeth were removed by the medical attendant. Wilkinson was found guilty 'of the most flagrant cruelty' and his licence was removed.

British asylums eventually abandoned the use of mechanical restraints to achieve order. Conolly (1856) lead the anti-restraint movement, popularising an alternative method of control: seclusion. The Metropolitan Commissioners in Lunacy (1844) had at an early point favoured seclusion:

> Seclusion is found to have a very powerful effect in tranquillizing, and subduing those who are under temporary excitement or paroxysms of violent insanity. As a temporary remedy, for very short periods, in case of paroxysms and of high excitement, we believe seclusion to be a valuable remedy.

The County Asylums with their rigidity and routine went further than simply using the control of a stronger force or threat of such a force, they disciplined their patients into their grand order by engendering self-control. The discipline of the Asylum partly depended on it being a total institution, isolated, self-sustaining, with its own rules and norms:

> ... since mental patients on the outside decline to respond to efforts at social control, there is the question of how social control is achieved on the inside. I believe it is achieved largely through the 'ward system', the means of control which has slowly evolved in modern mental hospitals. The key, I feel, is a system of wards graded for the degree of allowable misbehaviour and the degree of discomfort and depravation prevalent in them (Goffman 1961).

Asylum patients went through a system in which they became manageable, but at the price of reducing their individuality, drive and even self-identity. Ironically, such a state became known as institutional neurosis (Barton 1959); the treatment for the unmanageable had become a disease.

Discipline in psychiatric hospitals

Discipline is perhaps a more helpful description of the control currently operated by mental health professionals, since the aim of staff responses to unacceptable behaviour is to encourage the self-control of the patient, so that similar behaviour is avoided and that they may be eventually safely discharged into the community (Crichton 1995a). Better self-control, it will be argued, can be achieved through a variety of means including changes to medication, ward environment, etc. Rice *et al* (1989) comment:

> In order to reduce the amount of control that we potentially exert over a given individual, that individual must *acquire control over himself.* Thus in the long term, the goal of security and treatment is to have patients become their own monitors – to achieve control over their aggressive behaviors and exercise this control responsibly ... . The function of psychiatric or penal institutions is to maintain short-term control over potentially violent persons

while providing an environment conducive to their acquisition of self-control.

There is legal justification for the disciplining of the detained patient in England and Wales. The House of Lords ruled in the case of *Pountney* v. *Griffiths* (1976) that, implied in the power to detain a patient under mental health legislation, there was the right to 'control and discipline'. It is unclear, however, what that discipline should consist of. Gostin (1986) argues that the right to control and discipline could only be lawful for purposes intended in the Mental Health Act, i.e. health and safety, and that any discipline should be in a therapeutic spirit and should not include revenge or punishment.

The differentiation between acceptable discipline and unacceptable punishment is problematic: compulsorily detained patients might well consider their deprivation of liberty punishing in itself; and 'reward and punishment' are essential features of any behavioural treatment approach. There are, however, examples of unacceptable responses to patient violence described in recent public inquiries – for instance, in the case of Sean Walton described in the Ashworth Inquiry (DOH 1992), which found that the initial decision to seclude him after a violent incident was reasonable but that the decision to extend his seclusion the next day, after an entry in the nursing notes, 'no remorse for his actions', was punitive.

The mad/bad divide

A current popular notion is that there can be a division between the 'mad' and the 'bad' offender, the first being sent to hospital and the second to prison. It is perhaps easier for staff to respond to a violent incident when it has clearly been influenced by the patient's mental illness. Abnormal mental states, after all, are the familiar territory of psychiatric staff. However, patients are not readily characterised by a bad/mad dichotomy and some are capable of violence largely uninfluenced by mental disorder (of course badness and madness cannot be true alternatives since they come from distinct domains of discourse; the clinical and the moral). For example, a nurse was assaulted at an English regional secure unit by a patient well known to act violently in response to psychotic symptoms. The patient had some additional medication but no other sanction was placed on him. Later, full of remorse, the patient apologised to the nurse, telling him he had been bribed with cigarettes by another patient to commit the assault. From past experience the second patient expected the first would be treated more leniently than he would (I acknowledge the help of Dr Richard Byrt in this account).

A common impression is that the psychotically unwell are more often thought to be behaving under the influence of psychotic symptoms and to be 'mad', while patients diagnosed as having a personality disorder are thought to have more self-control and consequently their disruptive behaviour is regarded as 'bad'. This leads to the diagnosis of personality disorder readily being used in a prejudicial way (Lewis & Appleby 1988).

Martin (1984), in his review into psychiatric hospital inquiries, comments that violent patients can easily become the target of abuse, and that staff divide challenging behaviour into 'illness', which deserves care, and 'badness', which deserves punishment. Martin warns:

> The patient who is uncooperative, or who resists a particular form of treatment, can quickly be redefined as not deserving the best treatment. Informal punishment can come to be 'justified' as part of a process of teaching the patient to cooperate with the treatment and thereby become, if not actually cured, at least a better patient.

Martin goes on to quote Towell (1975):

> Perhaps the most important point here relates to the distinctions nurses make between those diagnostic characterisations which imply that the patient is 'ill' and those which do not. It seems clear that in this setting where the medical treatment ideology was a dominant influence that patients who are not regarded as 'ill' thereby lost their claim to receive help. Instead the deviant behaviour of such patients was likely to seem as intentioned, the deviant judged responsible, and attempts made to control the behaviour through the application of negative sanctions.

6. The Response to Psychiatric Inpatient Violence

In general psychiatry units informal patients are commonly discharged because of unacceptable behaviour. In the case of Christopher Clunis, his behaviour was at an early stage thought to have more to do with illicit drug use and his personality and less do do with psychotic illness (Ritchie 1994, ch. 4). In effect, his behaviour was thought of as being more 'bad' than 'mad', and he was abruptly discharged on several occasions after disturbed behaviour. Disturbed behaviour included masturbating openly, entering female dormitories, striking a patient and kicking a patient for no reason (Ritchie 1994, 4.3, 4.4). In a telephone conversation one of the doctors who had cared for Christopher Clunis gave the impression to a doctor, caring for him in another hospital, that there had been doubt about his diagnosis of schizophrenia and overall they thought he was a difficult young man who just wanted a bed. The hospital was unwilling to take responsibility for him because staff did not regard him as psychotic (Ritchie 1994, 6.2.2). The inquiry observed that the more disturbed Christopher Clunis became the less effective was his psychiatric care.

Maden (1993) comments that the mental health professional's rejection of the violent patient can be understood in the common feelings these patients elicit in staff: fear and helplessness. Maden (1993) goes on to consider whether a 'violence clinic' (Tennent & Wood 1990) which would pool expertise may be a positive response to the 'therapeutic nihilism' (Lewis 1974) that has 'often characterised psychiatry's response to violence' (Maden 1993).

Sanctions which are punitive do commonly exist and are often cloaked in therapeutic terms, such as 'over-correction therapy', used to describe the sanction of washing the floor in the case of Sean Walton (DOH 1993, p. 7). If sanctions are to have a place in hospital, then it needs to be clear what they are and when they are to be used, and there need to be safeguards and systems of appeal in place. One such approach is discussed in Chapter 7, where Richardson suggests the adoption of a formal disciplinary framework, particularly for use in maximum security special hospitals. Within the English special hos-

69

pitals many of the patients have been convicted of serious offences: Wong *et al* (1993) found that 55% of patients at Broadmoor Special Hospital had previous convictions for violent offences. The adoption of any disciplinary code would be challenging (Crichton 1995b). I favour the adoption of sanctions only within an integrated 'treatment response' rather than a system where there would need to be a decision between a 'treatment response' and a 'disciplinary response'.

A more helpful dichotomy?

The decision whether to use a treatment or disciplinary response after an incident of patient violence would involve a decision about the responsibility of the patient for his or her act. Any misdemeanour caused by a patient is likely to have arisen from a mixture of factors, some under his or her own determination, others influenced by the illness. This is a grey area of individual responsibility. It is notable that the factors behind psychiatric patient violence appear intimately linked to those behind violence generally, for example in Walker *et al*'s (1993) study which found similar rates for hospital psychiatric inpatient violence and violent crime rates and in Monahan's (1988) conclusion, that the best demographic predictors of violence are shared between the mentally disordered and non-mentally disordered. In a comprehensive study investigating the link between schizophrenia and crime Wessely *et al* (1994) found that the strongest associations of criminal conviction in schizophrenic subjects remained those recognised in non-schizophrenic subjects, although schizophrenia was found to increase risk of violent crime in men independently of other factors.

Perhaps a more helpful dichotomy is not whether a patient's act was 'mad or bad', but whether there is significant mental disorder present. If there is, then the gamut of behaviour the patient presents should be managed therapeutically. A sanction should not be cloaked in a therapeutic term, but a *reasonable* sanction, if subject to safeguards, could be used and seen as therapeutic in its own right.

6. The Response to Psychiatric Inpatient Violence

In the field of learning disabilities, Holland & Murphy (1990) describe a useful way of managing disturbed behaviour which recognises the complexity behind violent acts. They encourage the creation of a hypothesis to help understand why a particular behaviour is occurring and from that construct a management programme drawing from an appropriate blend of approaches. Such a blend might include talking therapy, medication change, change in the environment, or, as is suggested here, a reasonable sanction or the encouragement of reparation or apology (Crichton 1995b). To some extent such an approach is common sense and good practice, but the Blackwood Inquiry noted how staff failed to recognise the factor of Orville Blackwood's postponed Mental Health Review Tribunal in leading to the disturbed behaviour preceding his death (Prins 1993). In essence there is no substitute for 'knowing the patient'.

The acute management of a violent incident

There has been much debate about the management of violent incidents and in particular the use of medication, restraint and seclusion (Angold 1989, Grounds 1990, Hoggett 1985 Royal College of Psychiatrists 1990). The immediate task of management is simply to make a dangerous situation safe, although this cannot be completely separated from the more difficult decision of what to do next. There is growing consensus that the only role seclusion should play is in the acute management of a dangerous situation, for reasons of safety or to take the heat out an incident. The Metropolitan Commissioners in Lunacy gave enduring guidance in 1844 (see above).

The task of acute management may be straightforward, but its method is not. There is much divergence between clinicians about *how* a violent incident should be made safe. There are many different medications availiable, methods of manual restraint and styles of psychological intervention. In the heat of a dangerous situation and with different interventions availiable there is an increased risk of unsafe management. One solution is the adoption within individual units of guidelines or policies

71

on the acute management of behavioural disturbance. The guidelines at Fulbourn Hospital, Cambridge (Hunt & Gregory 1994) provide an example of good practice. They are agreed by local clinicians to suit the local population of patients, they are short enough not to overwhelm, and they strike a balance between flexibility of response and the laying down of safe management. Any local guidelines need to be regularly reviewed in the light of changes in patient population, clinical practice and medical audit.

Perhaps some of the problems which currently arise in the management of violence are generated by increased staff anxiety about assault (Crichton 1995a). In small psychiatric units, there is a greater reliance on portering staff or even the police to help contain patient violence. To avoid such situations occurring there is perhaps a growing reliance on prophylactic 'chemical restraint'.

The reporting of an incident and the role of the police

It is sometimes unclear to staff when to report an incident and what details to include and there is the need for national standards and guidelines. The review into the mental health services of South Devon Healthcare Trust (SDHT 1994) made important recommendations about the reporting of incidents. Scott-Moncreiff (1993) makes the point that incident reports may be very influential in the decisions made to discharge a patient, yet there are few safeguards to check their accuracy.

Incident reports should be used to review the safety of staff and the procedures in place to prevent and manage violence. The current Management of Health and Safety Regulations, in force since 1993 (Health and Safety Executive 1992) require hospitals to assess and measure the safety of staff, patients and visitors and to ensure adequate safety training for staff. Certain forms of training and certain uses of personal alarm may be counterproductive if they increase staff anxiety and confusion; staff should be given a true picture of the risks they face and be trained in the particular measures that will make their job safer.

6. The Response to Psychiatric Inpatient Violence

Staff do not inform the police about the vast majority of assaults which are of a minor nature. There may be a problem in using other patients as witnesses, outlined in the House of Lords ruling on *R* v. *Spencer* (1987). However, there seem to be three main circumstances when staff do inform the police of an incident:

- When the offence is judged serious, i.e. one which causes physical harm – but even in these circumstances, assaults which cause relatively major injury sometimes are not referred to the police; e.g. in the case of Orville Blackwood when the patient broke a nurse's jaw in an assault (Prins 1993).
- When a patient commits a minor criminal act which may be thought of as the precursor of a serious offence.
- When an offender patient is on a Hospital Order and commits an offence which is more serious than the index offence.

There is little British literature on this subject (Brand 1986, Drinkwater 1989). In a short report James (1989) surveyed 400 psychiatrists. 25% responded and of those, 40 had experience of initiating prosecution after an assault from a patient. Norko *et al* (1992) reviewed the subject in its American context and summarised the arguments for and against prosecution:

For:

(1) encourages patient responsibility and is therefore therapeutic (Schwarz & Greenfield 1978, Mills *et al* 1975, Stein & Diamond 1985);

(2) represents a type of reality therapy by limit-setting intervention (Miller & Maier 1987, Hoge & Gutheil 1987, Mills *et al* 1985, Rachlin 1982, Stein & Diamond 1985);

(3) improves staff morale and ability and willingness to treat violent patients (Miller & Maier 1987, Mills *et al* 1985, Rachlin 1982);

(4) deters violent behaviour (Phlen *et al*, 1985, Stein & Diamond 1985);

(5) allows for public scrutiny of violence in institutions (Phlen *et al*, 1985, Mills et al 1985);

(6) may be a just consequence for injurious acts. (Mills *et al* 1985).

Against:

(1) subverts the therapeutic alliance (Gutheil 1985);

(2) invites counter-suit by patients (Gutheil 1985);

(3) is an acting of counter transference on the part of the staff (Phlen *et al*, 1985);

(4) is impractical (Phlen *et al*, 1985);

(5) scapegoats patients for inadequacies in the treatment environment (Hoge & Gutheil 1987);

(6) may permanently alienate patients from the care system (Hoge & Gutheil 1987);

(7) may violate patient confidentiality (Gutheil 1985).

Norko *et al* (1992) and Appelbaum *et al* (1991) suggest that every psychiatric hospital should clearly have a policy on what offences the hospital should pursue as criminal prosecutions. There is confusion about when to involve the police, and there is a need for guidelines and agreements between managers, professional organisations and unions.

Supervision, surveillance and confidentiality

The case of Christopher Clunis in particular has highlighted the need for better community coordination and communication (Ritchie 1993, section V). Supervision registers with the necessary accompanying surveillance must be recognised as controlling in themselves (among others Foucault (1977) developed this theme). They take away a degree of confidentiality from the relationship between mental health professional and patient. Care in the community also brings into focus the difficulties of confidentiality when communicating to family members and other carers. The family is often essential in the care of the mentally disordered, especially when there is a history of violence, and they have particular rights and powers under the MHA 1983, but it still remains unclear who should be informed about a patient's violent behaviour.

Privileged information about a patient is usually shared among the team looking after him or her, and shared with third parties, including close family and carers, only with the express permission of the patient. It is already accepted that information may be shared freely with the Social Service members of multidisciplinary teams (DOH 1994), and perhaps there is a case for extending disclosure of confidential information to carers outside the Social Services, not only for reasons of overriding safety, but also to help plan community care. Government proposals about supervised discharge and supervision register challenge current conventions about confidentiality (DOH 1993 a and b respectively). Perhaps a more useful concept is respect for privileged information, in which patients know that, when there are good reasons, their psychiatric professionals may disclose to their carers, for instance, a violent incident in hospital or a threat.

The Mental Health Foundation Report (Utting 1994, pp. 57-9) highlights many of these points and recommends that the Department of Health issue fresh guidance on the protection of staff and carers. The report also comments on the death of Katy Sullivan (Utting 1994, p. 61), a psychology graduate tragically killed by a patient while she was working as a volunteer in a small hostel for the mentally disordered. The family strongly felt that a history of patient violence was not communicated by professionals to those who needed to know – specifically, the voluntary agencies. The family also felt that the follow-up with them, in terms of support and bereavement counselling was 'inadequate', and that they were 'insensitively handled'.

Care of the victim

Often the care of the victim or victim's family is forgotten. Staff support must recognise the fears of staff, and employers have a responsibility of care to staff who are assaulted. Some papers on the subject of staff victims and support include Anonymous 1985, Cauldwell 1992, Dawson *et al* 1988, Davies 1989, Hunter & Carmel 1992, Lanza 1983, 1992, Turnbull 1993, Whittington & Wykes 1989).

The Victim's Charter (Home Office 1990) makes the probation

service responsible for contacting and canvassing the opinion of the victim, or family of the victim, of life sentence offenders before their release. In the context of mentally disordered offenders the charter states: 'Everything will be done to avoid distress to victims or their relatives.' It is unclear what particular action agencies should take to avoid distress and it is unclear which agency, if any, is specifically responsible for considering the victim or victim's family upon the release of a mentally disordered offender. A recent release of a mentally disordered offender caused very great distress to the families of his victims (Ford 1994).

Summary

Recent public inquiries mark a shift in public concern about psychiatric control. Instead of criticising over control and abuse of power (Martin 1984), recent concern focuses on the under-control of psychiatry in the community (Ritchie 1994). There are dangers at both extremes, and psychiatric professionals must find a reasonable balance of care and control which meets public anxiety and respects patient autonomy.

One task of psychiatric control is to manage disturbed behaviour; it is suggested that the concepts of discipline and reasonable sanctions have a place within a therapeutic framework to manage such violence. There is a need for national guidance on the content and use of incident forms and the role of the police. There needs to be recognition that supervision and surveillance are forms of control and that developments in these areas require developments in the respect of professionals for privileged information.

References

ANGOLD A. (1989) Seclusion. *British Journal of Psychiatry* **154** 437-44.
ANONYMOUS (1985) Compensation for attacks by patients. *British Medical Journal* **291** 1496.
APPELBAUM K.L. & APPELBAUM P.S. (1991) A model hospital policy on

prosecuting patients for presumptively criminal acts. *Hospital and Community Psychiatry* **42** 1233-7.

BARTON R.W. (1959) *Institutional Neurosis*. Bristol: John Wright.

BRAND J. (1986) A fair cop. *Maudsley and Bethlem Gazette* **33** 24-5.

CALDWELL M.F. (1992) Incidence of PTSD among staff victims of patient violence. *Hospital and Community Psychiatry* **43** 838-9.

CLARE A. (1976) *Psychiatry in Dissent. Controversial Issues in Thought and Practice*. London: Tavistock.

CONOLLY J. (1856) *The Treatment of the Insane without Mechanical Restraint*. London: Smith and Elder.

CRICHTON J.H.M. (1995a) Psychiatric in-patient violence: issues of English law and discipline within hospitals. *Medicine, Science and the Law*. In press.

CRICHTON J.H.M. (1995b) Is it time for a formal disciplinary code for psychiatric in-patients in England and Wales? *Medicine, Science and the Law*. In press.

CULLEN (1780) *First Lines in the Practice of Physic*, vol. II. Edinburgh: Elliot, pp. 312-13.

DAWSON J., JOHNSTON M., KEHIAYAN N., KYANKO S. & MARTINEZ R. (1988) Response to patient and assault – a peer and support program for nurses. *Journal of Psychosocial Nursing and Mental Health Services* **26** 8-15.

DAVIES W. (1989) The prevention of assault on professional helpers. In K. Howells & C.R. Hollin (eds) *Clinical Approaches to Violence*. Chichester: John Wiley & Sons.

DOH (1992) *Report of the Committee of Inquiry into Complaints about Ashworth Hospital*, vol. II. Cm 2028-1. London: HMSO.

DOH (1993a) Press Release H93/908, 12 August.

DOH (1993b) Press Release H93/1144, 28 December.

DOH (1994) *Confidentiality, Use and Disclosure of Personal Health Information*. London: Department of Health, Para. 4.26.

DRINKWATER J. (1987) Violence in psychiatric hospitals. In K. Howells & C.R. Hollin (eds) *Clinical Approaches to Violence*. Chichester: John Wiley & Sons, p. 300.

FORD R. (1994) Relatives terrified of return. Killer who shot 5 freed to live near survivors. *The Times*, June 22, p. 5.

FOUCAULT M. (1977) *Discipline and Punish. The Birth of the Prison*. (tr. Alan Sheridan). London: Alan Lane.

GROUNDS A.T. (1990) Seclusion. In R. Bluglass and P. Bowden (eds) *Principles and Practice of Forensic Psychiatry*. Edinburgh: Churchill Livingstone, pp. 649-52.

GOFFMAN E. (1961) *Asylums. Essays on the Social Situation of Mental Patients and Other Inmates*. New York: Anchor Books, pp. 361-2.

GOSTIN L. (1986) *Mental Health Services – Law and Practice*. London: Shaw & Shaw Ltd.

GUTHEIL T.G. (1985) Prosecuting psychiatric patients. *Hospital and Community Psychiatry* **36** 1320-1.

HMSO (1990) *The Mental Health Act 1983 Code of Practice*, 2nd ed. London: HMSO, ch. 18.

HEALTH AND SAFETY EXECUTIVE (1992) *New Health and Safety at Work Regulations*. Sheffield: Health and Safety Executive.

HOLLAND T. & MURPHY G. (1990) Behavioural and psychiatric disorder in adults with mild learning difficulties. *International Review of Psychiatry* **2** 117-36.

HOGE S.K. & GUTHEIL T.G. (1987) The prosecution of psychiatric patients for assault on staff: a preliminary empirical study. *Hospital and Community Psychiatry* **36** 44-9.

HOGGETT B. (1985) Legal aspects of secure provision. In Gostin L. (ed.) *Secure Provision*. London: Tavistock, pp. 236-62.

HOME OFFICE (1990) *Victim's Charter. A Statement of the Rights of Victims of Crime*. London: Home Office, pp. 20-1.

HUNT N. & GREGORY C. (1994) *Guidelines for the Management of Acute Behavioural Disturbance*. Fulbourn Hospital, Cambridge: unpublished.

HUNTER M. & CARMEL H. (1992) The cost of staff injuries from inpatient violence. *Hospital and Community Psychiatry* **43** 586-8.

JAMES D.V. & COLLINGS S. (1989) Prosecuting psychiatric in-patients for violent acts: a survey of principles and practice. *Abstracts Annual Meeting London 4-6 July 1989, Psychiatric Bulletin* **Supp. 2** 60.

JONES K. (1993) *Asylums and After. A Revised History of the Mental Health Services: From the Early 18th Century to the 1900s*. London: Athlone.

LANZA M. (1983) The reactions by nursing staff to physical assault by a patient. *Hospital and Community Psychiatry* **34** 44-7.

LANZA M.L. (1992) Nurses as patient assault victims: an update, synthesis and recommendations. *Archives of Psychiatric Nursing* **6** 163-71.

LEWIS A. (1974) Psychopathic personality: a most elusive category. *Psychological Medicine* **4** 133-40.

LEWIS G. & APPLEBY L. (1988) Personality disorder: the patients psychiatrists dislike. *British Journal of Psychiatry* **153** 44-9.

LUNACY COMMISSION (1854) *Eighth Annual Report*. London: Lunacy Commission.

MACALPINE I. & HUNTER R. (1969) *George III and the Mad-business*. London: Penguin.

MADEN A. (1993) The psychiatric management of violence. In C. Thompson & P. Cowen (eds) *Violence. Basic and Clinical Science*. Oxford: Butterworth-Heinemann Ltd, p. 145.

MARKS J. (1994) The re-emergence of anti-psychiatry: psychiatry under threat. *Hospital Update* 187-9.

6. The Response to Psychiatric Inpatient Violence

MARTIN J. (1984) *Hospitals in Trouble.* Oxford: Basil Blackwell, esp. ch. 6.

METROPOLITAN COMMISSIONERS IN LUNACY (1844) *Report of the Metropolitan Commissioners in Lunacy to the Lord Chancellor.* London: Bradbury & Evans.

MILLER R.D. & MAIER G.J. (1987) Factors affecting the decision to prosecute mental patients for criminal behavior. *Hospital and Community Psychiatry* **38** 50-5.

MILLS M.J., PHELAN L.A. & RYAN J.A. (1985) In Reply (letter). *Hospital and Community Psychiatry* **36** 1321-2.

MONAHAN J. (1988) Risk assessment of violence among the mentally disordered: generating useful knowledge. *International Journal of Law and Psychiatry* **11** 249-57.

NORKO M.A., ZONAN H.V. & PHILIPS R.T.M. (1992) Prosecuting assaultive psychiatric patients. *Journal of Forensic Science* **3** 923-31.

PARRY-JONES W. (1972) *The Trade in Lunacy.* London: Routledge and Kegan Paul.

PHELAN L.A., MILLS M.J. & RYAN J.A. (1985) Prosecuting psychiatric patients for assault. *Hospital and Community Psychiatry* **36** 581-2.

PORTER R. (1987) *Mind-Forg'd Manacles: A History of Madness in England from the Restoration to the Regency.* London: Athlone.

PRINS H. (Chairman) (1993) *Report of the Committee of Inquiry into the Death in Broadmoor Hospital of Orville Blackwood and a Review of the Deaths of Two Other Afro-Caribbean Patients. 'Big, Black and Dangerous?'.* London: SHSA.

RACHLIN S. (1982) Towards a definition of staff rights. *Hospital and Community Psychiatry* **33** 60-1.

ROYAL COLLEGE OF PSYCHIATRISTS (1990) The seclusion of psychiatric patients. *Psychiatric Bulletin* **14** 754-6.

RICE M.E., HARRIS G.T., VARNEY G.W. & QUINSEY V.L. (1989) *Violence in Institutions. Understanding, Prevention and Control.* Toronto: Hogrefe & Huber, p. 105.

RITCHIE J.H. (Chairman) (1994) *Report of the Inquiry into the Care and Treatment of Christopher Clunis.* London: HMSO.

SAUNDERS T.J. (ed.) (1970) *Plato: The Laws.* London: Penguin, pp. 376-8, 481-2.

SCHWARZ C.J. & GREENFIELD G.P. (1978) Charging a patient with assault of a nurse on a psychiatric unit. *Canadian Psychiatric Association Journal* **4** 197-200.

SCOTT-MONCREIFF L. (1993) Injustice in forensic psychiatry. *Journal of Forensic Psychiatry* **4** 97-108.

SOUTH DEVON HEALTHCARE TRUST (1994) *Report of the Review into the Mental Health Services of South Devon Healthcare Trust.* Torquay: South Devon Healthcare Trust, pp. 56-7.

STEIN L.I. & DIAMOND R.J. (1985) The chronically ill and the criminal

79

justice system: when to call the police. *Hospital and Community Psychiatry* **36** 271-4.

SZASZ T.S. (1961) *The Myth of Mental Illness: Foundations of a Theory of Personal Conduct*. New York: Dell.

TANTUM D. (1991) The anti-psychiatry movement. In G.E. Berrios & H. Freeman (eds) *150 years of British Psychiatry, 1841-1991*. London: Gaskell, for the Royal College of Psychiatrists.

TENNENT G. & WOOD R. (1990) The management of violence. In R. Bluglass & P. Bowden (eds) *Principles and Practice of Forensic Psychiatry*. London: Churchill Livingstone, pp. 653-68.

TOWELL D. (1975) *Understanding Psychiatric Nursing*. London: Royal College of Nursing.

TUKE (1813) *Description of the Retreat, an Institution near York*, repr. R. Hunter & I. MacAlpine (eds) (1964). London: Dawsons.

TURNBULL J. (1993) Victim support. *Nursing Times* **89** 33-4.

UTTING W. (Chairman) (1994) *Creating Community Care. Report of the Mental Health Foundation Inquiry into Community Care for People with Severe Mental Illness*. London: Mental Health Foundation.

WALKER N. (1968). *Crime and Insanity in England*. Edinburgh: Edinburgh University Press.

WALKER W.D. & CAPLAN R.P. (1993) Assaultive behaviour in acute psychiatric wards and its relationship to violence in the community: a comparison of two health districts. *Medicine, Science and the Law* **33** 300-4.

WESSELY S.C., CASTLE D., DOUGLAS A.J. & TAYLOR P.J. (1994) The criminal careers of incident cases of schizophrenia. *Psychological Medicine* **24** 483-502.

WING J.K. (1978) *Reasoning about Madness*. Oxford: Oxford University Press.

WHITTINGTON R. & WYKES T. (1989) Invisible injury. *Nursing Times* **85** 30-2.

WONG M., LUMSDEN J., FENTON G. & FENWICK P. (1993) Violence ratings of Special Hospital patients. *Journal of Forensic Psychiatry* **4** 471-80

Cases

Pountney v. *Griffiths* [1976] A.C. 314.

R. v. *Spencer and Others* [1987] A.C. 128, 137.

Managerial and Nursing Perspectives on the Response to Inpatient Violence

Lorraine Conlon, Andrew Gage and Tony Hillis

Introduction

In 1974 the Government, following the recommendations of the Butler Report (Department of Health and Home Office 1975), agreed to set up regional medium secure units within the NHS, to fill the gap between maximum security provision and open hospitals. The aim of this programme was to provide comprehensive and specialised health services for an increasing number of mentally disordered offenders in the criminal justice system. These new units established programmes which provided assessment, treatment and rehabilitation in conditions of medium security. Reaside Clinic was opened in October 1987 to meet this need in the West Midlands Region.

General philosophy

The main function of the West Midlands Forensic Service is to provide assessment, care and treatment.

> Within the constraints of the law, potential for dangerousness towards others and the need for their protection, a user of the services should have the same liberty, rights, autonomy and choice as any other member of the community (Reaside Clinic 1987).

Management philosophy

The development and operation of the Forensic Service is led by the Clinical Director, supported by the Director of Nursing and Operational Services. Daily running of the service is managed at all levels within the organisation so as to ensure that the interests of users are given foremost consideration. All management decisions are made, as far as is possible, in an open manner, with full discussion and consultation with the personnel involved.

Range of services

Inpatient services

Inpatient services at Reaside Clinic are divided into different functional units, each offering highly specialised services designed to match the individual needs of patients. The functions of each of the units are as follows:

- in-depth/specialist assessments to determine the most appropriate approach to care;
- short-term holistic assessment and treatment of acute mental illness;
- intensive psychiatric care for patients requiring high levels of staffing, interaction and observation;
- therapeutic community techniques to enable rehabilitation, and to enable the patient to accept various responsibilities;
- cognitive behavioural therapy to encourage a change of beliefs associated with maladaptive patterns of behaviour and emotion;
- living skills assessment and development to assist the patients in acquiring survival skills and equip them with the necessary confidence and practical knowledge to live in the community.

The transfer of patients from one residential unit to another is based upon individual need. Movement between areas is viewed by patients as a natural progression along the treatment path.

To support residential units there are a wide variety of group and individual programmes, based in a large, well equipped resource centre comprising a multi-purpose gymnasium, workshop, and a variety of craft, education and group rooms. Although it is not residential, the rehabilitation resource area provides a further functional unit. This open and easily accessible place comprises areas designed to facilitate activities of daily living, pre-vocational training, education sports and recreation. Structured multi-professional activity takes place within this area until 9 pm during the week, but it is available to staff and patients on a 24-hour basis. The activities are determined by the needs of the patients with each planning his/her own programme under the guidance of the key worker and occupational therapist.

Response to aggression

In considering responses to aggression, it is vitally important to examine the role played by professionals in preventing or minimising potential aggression in any health care setting. Patients resident in secure accommodation are often seen as having more potential for aggression, or as behaving in a more violent manner, than patients in a more open setting. This is not necessarily the case at Reaside Clinic where there is a high level of staff-patient contact. Staff are aware, however, of the high level of staff-patient contact making nurses a prime target for violence when it does occur (Shuttleworth 1989).

One of the most important aspects of the management of violence and aggression in a secure unit is not control or security, but the provision of an environment which encourages and actively promotes open discussion of feelings. Further to this, respecting the individual patient as a person and enabling detained patients to have as much responsibility for their own lives as possible are both integral to the management of violence and aggression.

A study by Lowe (1992) suggests the following categories of effective intervention used by psychiatric nurses when faced with challenging behaviour:

- confirming messages
- personal control
- staff honesty
- providing face-saving alternatives
- setting limits

- use of structure
- facilitating expression
- monitoring
- timing
- calming
- use of non-verbal skills

Staff employed within Reaside Clinic are encouraged to be aware of and utilise such interventions.

Prevention of aggression

Prevention of aggression actually begins with appropriate recruitment and selection of staff. A patient with a considerable history of aggression towards staff, indicated to staff that he considered that the best nurses were those that show, by their attitude, a respect for the service user. He identified, in particular, with one nurse whom he said would always talk 'to the part of me which isn't neurotic or mad'. He was effectively indicating that the nurse always treated him with dignity and respect.

Lowe's study from 1992 acknowledges dignity and respect as important characteristics in members of the caring profession. At Reaside Clinic, emphasis is placed not only on ability and professional qualifications, but also on attitude and personality. The personal qualities desired of staff working within Reaside Clinic are those of flexibility, warmth, clarity in communication, a demonstrable non-judgemental approach and a patient-focused approach. It is important that staff remain calm in difficult circumstances, react positively when faced with aggression, and also accept that patients have a right to display their feelings, even if it is done in an inappropriate manner, as long as there is no direct risk to themselves or anybody else. Staff are encouraged to adopt a flexible approach to the management of difficult patients, creating individual and innovative care programmes and plans based on individual need. Care programmes reflect a non-judgemental approach, and management of potential violence or aggression involves a range of required skills as outlined by Argyle (1975), Ekman & Friesen (1979) and Izard (1971). All these authors examined the ability of the nurse to recognise the emotion the patient feels and the threat the patient may perceive as being posed. Skills required by the nurse include self-awareness, appropriate use of posture, intention movements, eye contact, proximity, orientation, touch, facial and vocal cues and appearance.

The use of rules and regulations, however, may be of less value than a more general self-awareness. This is partly because of the difficulty of recalling such conceptual injunctions in tense situations requiring rapid responses. The use of touch may have a calming effect in some instances, but it may be misinterpreted by some as an invasion of space and thus be perceived as provocation. Farrell (1992) states that:

> Carers should examine how they may have contributed to the patient's angry outburst and should bear in mind, regardless of who is at fault, that the satisfactory conclusion of encounters depends on the interpersonal skills of the nurse.

Sensitivity to non-verbal cues of others, and an awareness of the presentation of self were described by Lowe (1992) as important factors in the recognition and defusing of aggression.

Training is seen as paramount in providing competence and confidence in the staff's response to aggression. This begins with the staff induction programme, where trainees, who may or may not have been faced with aggression before, are encouraged to examine the patient's role in aggression, and to consider how their own values and behaviour play a role in preventing it.

Regular training is provided for staff within the clinic, so that they are refreshed on policies relating to, for example, restraint procedures, attack alarm use, observation and breakaway techniques. It is also an important opportunity for staff to review their own attitudes and values, and to discuss any issues they consider to be important.

As part of staff development, qualified staff within Reaside Clinic attend a professional development programme, addressing various areas of personal and professional competence and skill. The programme was developed within Reaside so as to suit the needs of those working within the forensic service. Based on a modular principle it covers broad areas of management, clinical, research and forensic issues. Staff attend sessions that suit their individual needs, unit requirements and clinic needs. Attendance is recorded and certificated so as to provide evidence of regular professional updating.

The control and restraint course run by Reaside Clinic places emphasis not only on physical skills, but on psychological intervention and verbal skills, giving priority to prevention and early identification of the potential for aggression. It is a three-week course based around six modules:

- communication skills
- problem solving
- safe management of aggressive incidents
- effects of chemotherapy
- emotional and supportive needs of staff
- the role of early identification in potentially aggressive situations

The course philosophy states:

> The use of any physical intervention is considered a last resort and should only be used when all other interventions have been tried and failed, and/or an individual's behaviour demonstrates that they are likely to cause harm (West 1993).

The underlying principle in training is to allow participants to examine themselves as well as look at the behaviour of others. Attitudes and preventative issues are key areas around which all other aspects of the training are constructed.

Techniques of control and restraint are not viewed in isolation, but compliment other skills that staff utilise in this difficult and challenging aspect of care. These courses contain theoretical and physical components which are both taught and experiential.

Through the generation of such an environment as has been described earlier, a culture has developed within Reaside Clinic which contributes greatly to the proactive approach to managing aggression and the subsequent minimising of aggression. Reaside Clinic's philosophy supports the view and belief that security and therapy should be equally balanced (Figure 1).

Figure 1. The relationship between security and a therapeutic environment

This figure represents the Reaside philosophy concerning the relationship between security and a therapeutic environment: a balance. If security is raised, therapeutic levels reduce and *vice versa*.

Reaside Clinic uses advances in technology to minimise obtrusive physical security measures. The Clinic doors are 'hands free', opened by small access cards placed unobtrusively in a pocket. Such devices make the use of keys and chains unnecessary, moving away from a custodial approach in the care setting. Support is also given in the provision of personal attack alarms, thus ensuring that staff are always able to summon assistance in a crisis. The alarm system is monitored by reception staff, and a public address system announces where staff are required in the event of an alarm being set off. Staff on each residential unit are allocated to respond to these alarms, and can be on the scene within seconds.

Reaside Clinic's philosophy reflects care for patients on an individual basis. This involves the involvement of patients as much as possible in their care through care planning and advocating for the patient in weekly nursing summaries. Further to this, individual handovers are held with each patient, empowering the patients to challenge nurse perceptions and observations and have their point of view recorded.

Nursing assessment will examine any history of aggressive behaviour with a view to ensuring proactive care planning and appropriate placement within the clinic. Such assessments will be carried out in many circumstances by a patient's potential keyworker before admission, so as to enable a familiar face to be available at the time of admission.

Emphasis is also placed on knowing the patient. It is of paramount importance that the staff spend large amounts of time with the patients, so as to gather relevant information and establish a therapeutic relationship. Unit teams on the residential units are divided into care groups, and nurses from a patient's group are allocated accordingly as a way of ensuring consistency of care. Groups are supervised by a unit manager, who monitors prescribed care, ensuring that it incorporates the overall philosophy. In addition to this senior nurses, as members of clinical teams, are responsible for overseeing the prescribed care and how it is implemented with their respective patients.

As well as developing a positive culture, which includes ensuring that as much privacy, dignity and responsibility are given to the patient as possible, staff are encouraged to develop positive approaches to managing challenging behaviour. This means an acceptance of incidents which go against one's natural inclinations, e.g. accepting damage to furniture or property as a patient's way of expressing emotion. Actions such as these can be used later in order to highlight inappropriate behaviour and set out a more appropriate way to examine actions in the future, as well as to examining the expression of anger and frustration.

Skill mix is an important aspect of preventing or managing aggression, and qualified nurses are encouraged to develop skills so as to manage resources effectively, to ensure that experienced staff are available to provide input to distressed patients. This could mean that many members of the clinical team are used to provide input at times of crisis, as well as to recognise antecedents and to decide on appropriate intervention to minimise or prevent aggressive incidents.

Care is taken to ensure that patients in Reaside Clinic are aware of their rights under the Mental Health Act (MHA) 1983, and aware of the complaints procedure. A full-time clinical records officer is employed within Reaside Clinic with particular responsibility for this.

The role of senior managers in the clinic involves ensuring that training and development opportunities are maintained and that appropriate policies and procedures are in place and adhered to, providing advice support and guidance to staff on dealing with incidents, and monitoring documentation and standards. Senior managers have an overall responsibility in ensuring that staff maintain a positive approach to the management of difficult patients. They are clinically involved with patients, providing a link between staff and clinical teams. Formal and informal staff appraisal is an ongoing process aiming to develop strengths and overcome weaknesses in performance. Development of staff is not through education alone; it is imperative that regular feedback is given to staff through clinical supervision. In this way general issues of conduct and appropriate and inappropriate use of terminology can be addressed, essential in the maintenance of a therapeutic atmosphere.

Senior nursing staff have a responsibility to follow up complaints of unfair treatment, and to ensure that responses to complaints reach the patients quickly and effectively. Following aggressive incidents managers are responsible for providing support and debriefing to staff, and for helping identify areas that can be improved in handling crises.

Reaside has developed guidelines for the use of prn medication (as required), laying out criteria for its administration, ensuring that it is given in line with treatment plans and the MHA Code of Practice (HMSO 1993), and does not exceed agreed limits in second opinion documentation. All medication is given following assessment by medical staff.

Follow-up and after-care

Most of the patients residing in Reaside Clinic are moving towards discharge into the community at some point and will be familiar with the community staff who will be co-ordinating their care when they leave.

It is important that the CFPN (Community Forensic Psychiatric Nurse) and the social worker are introduced to the patient as soon as possible following admission. This not only familiarises them with the members of the clinical team responsible for their after-care, but promotes a positive attitude to their life after Reaside, and the need to plan future care under the care programme approach.

Patients are given the opportunity, through informal discussion with the CFPN and more formally through case conferences, to express their needs and wishes and thus can take some responsibility for their care. The CFPN is in a prime position to assess the home or hostel environment and to support carers by providing them with the appropriate information and education about mental illness. This is an ideal opportunity for the CFPN to build a relationship with both patient and carers, which can minimise acute stress at times of crisis. The care plans account for the carers' needs and are geared towards the recognition of early signs of illness and appropriate intervention and monitoring.

Reaside recognises the need for an instant response mechanism in the community in much the same way that it responds to crises and aggressive outbursts within the Clinic. At all times a CFPN and a social worker are on call to respond to crises which may occur in the community. This is 24-hour year-round cover, and has the back-up of on-call staff within the Clinic, such as a duty doctor, a duty consultant or a duty senior nurse.

Most emergency services for the mentally ill advise their patients to use their GP as a first point of contact. In a study by Lee (1990), it was found that the majority of psychiatrists (84%) felt that they should screen all requests for out-of-hours assistance. This would serve to screen out inappropriate calls, which they felt went particularly to GPs. If, for example, the patient or carer is expected to pass the first contact, the GP, and to be subsequently passed on from the second contact, the psychiatrist, much anxiety and distress can result along with a general waste of time, when the essence of crisis intervention is instant response.

The Clunis Report (Ritchie 1994) recommended collaborative initiatives, but without instant response teams we are in danger of further tragedies occurring when mentally ill people reach crisis point and are unable to access immediate help.

Reaside community staff are contacted directly by the patient or carer, through the reception staff at Reaside. All carry bleeps and mobile telephones in order to respond. It is clinic policy that all requests are dealt with at the time of referral and not postponed for a routine 9-5 hours.

Some of the crisis calls are requests from police stations for assessment as a result of behaviour that has brought the patient to the attention of the general public or police officers. The CFPN department provides a service not only to police stations, with advice and early intervention (Wix 1994), but to the courts, when a mentally disordered offender has been charged and requires diversion from the criminal justice system into the appropriate health care setting (Hillis 1993).

A case study

The nature of the problem.

Mr Smith (name changed) is a 30-year-old man who was admitted to the Clinic from his local psychiatric service following a serious assault on a fellow resident. He was initially admitted to our intensive care facility following a pre-admission assessment. He has a long history of mental health problems and on previous admissions had made serious assaults on fellow residents and nursing staff.

On admission, he was described as being pleasant and amiable. However, he was expressing ideas that he was a bodyguard to the Queen. He was reported to have been irritable, being in conflict with other residents on the unit, clenching his fists, expressing the idea that he hated 'nonces'. Over the coming weeks, Mr Smith's mental state continued to deteriorate, to the extent that he was making verbal threats when he perceived that his needs were not met. This resulted in him carrying out assaults on other patients. He was exhibiting acute psychotic symptoms on a regualr basis. He was demanding and becoming aggressive when demands were not met. He would frequently refuse medication.

Staff response

Mr Smith's keyworker formulated care plans to manage both his mental illness and his aggressive behaviour. These care plans ensured that staff followed a consistent approach when interacting with Mr Smith and that consistent data were gathered and forwarded to the patient's clinical team. Mr Smith was reviewed weekly by the full team, but they were available in the intervening period should any problems arise.

The staff took a firm approach in managing Mr Smith's aggressive behaviour. They did not give in to threats, but listened to him and allowed him to express his feelings openly. When Mr Smith demanded more freedom within the Clinic, the staff compromised by increasing his levels of leave within the Clinic but increasing the escort level to reflect the fact that he was not sufficiently well to have the total freedom he requested. The staff would engage him in conversation and an individual programme of activities was drawn up to divert him from his abnormal thought processes.

During the assessment, it was discovered that Mr Smith responded positively to female members of staff. Female staff were therefore used to intervene, particularly when Mr Smith was hostile or aggressive. One example of this occurred when Mr Smith broke pieces of wood from a chair and threatened male staff with them. He was approached by a female member of staff and he handed over the wood to her.

It was also noted that Mr Smith responded well to input from members of the clinical team, and regular visits to the unit were made by the senior nurse and medical staff of his particular team. This encouraged Mr Smith to feel involved in his care, and he had the opportunity to discuss his care regularly with people he felt were influential in making decisions about his future.

One particular incident illustrates clearly how the approaches we have discussed can be successful in minimising aggression. Mr Smith was detained under the MHA 1983. Owing to his disturbed behaviour and the clear indications of severe mental illness, it was decided that his section should be renewed. Mr Smith was extremely upset by this and walked out into the secure courtyard of the intensive care unit, where he proceeded to smash numerous windows with stones that he picked up from the garden. Staff activated the alarm system and responded quickly to the situation. It was decided to leave Mr Smith in the courtyard as he was secure and isolated from other patients and presented no risk to anyone. Staff maintained contact with him from outside the courtyard and continued to talk to him while he worked through his anger. Once the situation had been resolved and Mr Smith had calmed down, staff were able to discuss the incident with him and review his feelings. Members of staff recognised that he was still extremely ill and that he was not totally in control of his actions. They were also able to discuss their own feelings, conduct a full debriefing of the incident and identify potential areas for improvement or actions that had proved successful, thus learning as much as possible from the situation.

Gertz (1980) emphasises the importance of allowing time for teams to discuss critical incidents in the context of their overall philosophy. He describes how unstructured open-ended interviews with fifteen staff members (nominated for their effectiveness in defusing violent behaviour) were used to identify the components of successful interventions. The categories which Gertz and his associates obtained in this way were as follows: personal control, staff honesty, use of structure, assessment, alternatives and choice, use of touch and positive reinforcement.

Over the next few weeks, with more intensive support and an active medication regime, Mr Smith gradually became more settled and was able to move to a less secure rehabilitation unit, where he continued to make steady progress. His medication was gradually reduced until a therapeutic level was reached, and his rehabilitation needs are currently being addressed.

Conclusion

The management of aggressive behaviour lies mainly in providing a pro-active environment. The emphasis is on prevention rather than control of aggressive behaviour, and on development of a culture that encourages openness and the empowerment of patients to control their own lives.

We recognise that incidents of aggression will occur despite positive use of nursing intervention. At these times, the emphasis should be on returning the situation to normal as soon as possible, maintaining communication, dignity and respect for the individual, yet at the same time recognising the need for staff to feel supported and valued.

The Clinic continues to review its management of challenging behaviour and is always seeking to develop new approaches to care, to seek innovative and dynamic fields of research, to share ideas and to develop and promote good practice.

We have shown in this chapter that, given good managerial support, adequate resources, attention to staff training and development, the flexibility and motivation to move forward, and the ability to be open-minded and self-critical, it is possible to provide high quality care to difficult client groups in a relaxed and therapeutic atmosphere.

References

ARGYLE M. (1975) *Bodily Communication*. London: Methuen.
DEPARTMENT OF HEALTH AND HOME OFFICE (1975) *Report of the Committee on Mentally Abnormal Offenders*. Comd 6244 (The Butler Report). London: HMSO.
EKMAN P. & FRIESEN W.V. (1979) Measuring facial movements. In S.

7. Managerial and Nursing Perspectives

Weitz (ed.) *Non Verbal Communication*. Oxford: Oxford University Press.

FARRELL G. (1992) Therapeutic response to verbal aggression. *Nursing Standard* **6** (47) p. 31.

GERTZ B. (1980) Training for prevention of assaultative behaviour in a psychiatric setting. *Hospital and Community Psychiatry* **31** 628-30.

HMSO (1993) *The Mental Health Act Code of Practice*. 2nd ed. London: HMSO.

HILLIS G. (1993) Diverting tactics. *Nursing Times* **89** No. 1.

IZARD C.E. (1971) *The Face of Emotion*. New York: Appleton-Century-Crofts.

LEE H. (1990) Out of hours work by CPNs. In C. Brooker (ed.) *Community Psychiatric Nursing. A Research Perspective*. London: Chapman and Hall, p. 187.

LOWE T. (1992) Characteristics of effective nursing interventions in the management of challenging behaviour. *Journal of Advanced Nursing* **17** 1226-32.

REASIDE CLINIC (1987) *Philososphy Document. Charter of Rights for Patients in the Forensic Service*. The Reaside Clinic, Birmingham: unpublished.

RITCHIE J.H. (Chairman) (1994) *The Report of the Inquiry into the Care and Treatment of Christopher Clunis*. London: HMSO.

SHUTTLEWORTH A. (1989) Violence: is enough being done to protect you? *Professional Nurse* **Feb**. 227-8.

WEST M. (1992) *Therapeutic Intervention of Aggression Incorporating Control and Restraint Techniques. Course Philosophy*. The Reaside Clinic, Birmingham: unpublished.

WIX S. (1994) Keeping on the straight and narrow. *Psychiatric Care* **1** 102.

Openness, Order and Regulation in a Therapeutic Setting

Genevra Richardson

This chapter develops and applies an argument that I have presented in more general terms elsewhere (Richardson 1993). It seeks to establish a case for formalising and regulating the investigative and disciplinary processes which already occur within psychiatric hospitals, and offers, by way of illustration, a skeletal document in the form of a draft hospital policy governing the detaining authority's reporting of and response to seriously disruptive behaviour on the part of detained patients. The policy is designed to ensure that any response on the part of the authority is justified, therapeutically sound and fairly applied. By way of introduction I set out briefly the reasoning behind the position adopted and then consider some important points raised by the attempt to put such reasoning into practice.

The case for regulation

Disruptive behaviour occurs from time to time on any psychiatric ward. As other contributors to this volume report (Chapters 5 and 6), psychiatric patients can be frightening, violent and hard to control, and the detaining authorities will and must respond. Sometimes immediate action is necessary to protect person or property. Of greater concern here, however, is the more considered response to disruptive behaviour.

An example may help to illustrate the issue: a male patient hits a member of the education staff. Action may be needed immediately to defuse the situation and, depending on the policies operating within the hospital, the patient may be secluded or taken back to the ward and 'talked down' by a nurse. In addition, if the patient has behaved in a similar way before, the clinical team may think that he should be confined to the ward for a week. Several alternative justifications might be presented for such action, ranging from therapeutic, to protective, to punitive, or any combination of the three. If the patient is briefly secluded the justification might be entirely protective of the patient or of others; but if the seclusion is allowed to continue a little longer than is strictly necessary for protective purposes the desire to teach the patient a lesson might have intervened. Similarly, if the patient is confined to the ward his confinement might be thought necessary to protect others, or it might be part of a well structured treatment plan; on the other hand it might be designed to punish or deter. Indeed different members of the clinical team might emphasise different justifications for their actions.

Whatever the reasons behind them, however, the actions taken by the clinical team in response to violent and disruptive behaviour will interfere with the interests of the patient. If a detained patient who has been accustomed to wandering freely about the hospital is confined to his ward, his residual liberty will be significantly curtailed and his quality of life adversely affected. In any situation where a 'public' authority interferes with the interests of an individual, society is entitled to demand that such interference is justified: that it is related to a proper purpose and is taken in the public interest in the broadest sense (Richardson 1993). The interests of detained patients have already been significantly curtailed, and society (through the Mental Health Act 1983) must be assumed to have authorised that interference, presumably for the purposes of treatment and/or the protection of either the patient or others (MHA 1983 Sections 3, 37, 41). However, while the MHA expressly authorises detention in hospital and compulsory treatment (Section 58), it does not concern itself with the authority for many of the decisions taken in hospital which affect the residual interests of patients. Authority for these decisions must be found in the general objects of treatment and protection.

According to even the narrowest of definitions, treatment and protection must be understood to justify, for example, action taken in conformity with an agreed treatment plan, or the denial of free movement about the hospital to a persistent absconder. But their scope cannot rest there. Hospital authorities are required to detain patients against their will and at the same time to function as a therapeutic environment safe for patients, staff and visitors. In order to enable them to perform this task the authorities must be able to set some rules of conduct and to react, punitively if necessary, to any breach. Provided any such punitive or disciplinary action is reasonable there is now broad agreement that it would be lawful according to domestic law (Gostin 1986, Hoggett 1990, *Pountney* v. *Griffiths* 1976). Subject to certain provisos, some of which are mentioned below, it would also seem to meet the requirements of the European Convention for the Protection of Human Rights and Fundamental Freedoms (ECHR) and thus be acceptable by international legal standards as well.

Once the notion of discipline is mentioned in a hospital context, with all the connotations it carries of accusations, findings of guilt and cumbersome procedures, problems arise and old enmities re-emerge. It places in sharp relief the conflict between legalism and the therapeutic endeavour which is thought to underlie the history of the law's involvement in the regulation of mental health care (Rose 1985, Unsworth 1987, Peay 1989). According to this characterisation psychiatry is striving to do good, to treat, to act in the patient's best interests; while the law is concerned to do what is correct in a more formal sense. Too much legal regulation will be counter-productive and will inhibit the therapeutic goal. I want to break down this crude polarity and dispel the belief that any recognition of a disciplinary code and introduction of the accompanying process requirements would lead to sterile legalism.

The argument starts from the assumption that disciplinary

sanctions which interfere with the residual freedoms of detained patients are already imposed in psychiatric hospitals, but that they are imposed informally (HMSO 1992). According to the present argument such sanctions can be justified in a substantive sense, and their implementation can facilitate the treatment objective rather than being hostile to it. A detaining authority is required to detain and treat patients and in order to do so it can legitimately establish rules of conduct and sanctions, but the way in which it does this is of crucial importance.

In the first place the rules of conduct must be properly devised. If the rules are to be justified they must be directly related to the detaining authority's duty to maintain safety and control and to operate as a hospital, and the sanctions must be appropriate to that goal. In European terms they must be proportionate (Boyle 1994). Ideally the authority for the rules should be provided by statute while their details could be agreed locally. The inclusion of statutory authority would provide both the opportunity for some public debate of the principles at stake and, as far as is possible under our present constitutional system, some democratic legitimation of the scheme. It would also ensure compliance with the 'according to law' requirements of the ECHR (Articles 6(2) and 8(2)). Once the principles are established by statute the details of the rules could be devised locally in consultation with the patients. Far from being counter-therapeutic, such a process would promote an open discussion of the limits of acceptable behaviour.

Secondly, the rules must be fairly and accurately applied. If a breach is suspected the process of investigation must be open, independent and participative. The patient must be involved at every stage. Such a procedure should not be regarded as cumbersome and legalistic; by being open and by encouraging the patient to participate it would be facilitative of the treatment objective not hostile to it. It should also lead to more accurate decision-making. An investigative process which requires the open presentation and testing of evidence should encourage accurate findings of fact (Bayles 1990). Not only would this ensure that each individual response to suspected violence, for example, was justified, but of equal importance it would also improve the accuracy with which incidents are reported on a patient's notes. The accurate reporting of problem behaviour is essential for diagnostic and predictive purposes. Any assessment of a patient's suitability for transfer, discharge etc. will be significantly influenced by reports appearing on the notes. It is essential both in fairness to the patient and in fairness to society at large that these reports be as accurate as possible.

Finally, before considering the issues raised by any attempt to implement these ideas, it is important to remember that the discussion is concerned with mentally disordered patients, and that in some cases the notion of discipline may be entirely inappropriate. The patient may be very ill and the disruptive behaviour at issue may spring directly from that illness (see Chapter 6). However, this will not always be the case, and even where it is partly so the appropriate response may still be disciplinary. Further, even when the appropriate response is therapeutic not punitive, it is still essential that all concerned know what has been decided and why, and it is just as important that a proper investigation into the facts is conducted. The arson attempt, whatever its origins and however ill the patient concerned, must be accurately attributed. The procedure discussed below can deal with both a punitive and a therapeutic response. It does not presuppose punishment nor does it rest the choice of response on questions of individual responsibility where these are inappropriate.

A draft policy

The text of the policy is produced in full below, followed by discussion of various points arising from it.

THE REPORTING OF AND RESPONSE TO DISRUPTIVE BEHAVIOUR ON THE PART OF PATIENTS

Object
The object of this policy document is to set out a procedure to enable the detaining authority to respond to seriously disruptive

or disturbing behaviour on the part of detained patients in a fair and therapeutic manner.

Scope
The policy applies to all cases where detained patients are suspected of involvement in any of the following:
(a) fire setting;
   assault;
   use or possession of proscribed drugs;
   possession of a weapon.
(b) possession of pornographic, sadistic or morbid material;
   sexually threatening behaviour.

Operation
Where a detained patient is suspected of any of the above no report of the incident will be recorded on the patient's clinical notes, subject to the exception specified below, and no staff response beyond that immediately required to protect person or property will be initiated until a charge inquiry has been held. Where in the case of a suspected criminal offence it is thought appropriate to refer the matter to the police, the fact of that reference shall be recorded in the patient's notes.

Notice
In all cases where the decision is taken not to call in the police, or the police are unable to pursue the matter, the RMO (Responsible Medical Officer) will inform the patient of the nature of the allegation made and of the fact that it will be inquired into by an investigator. The procedure will be explained to the patient who will be informed that he or she may be accompanied to the inquiry by an advocate.

The independent investigator
The hospital will appoint a manager to act as an investigator in all cases where a serious allegation is made. In less serious cases an investigator may be appointed from the staff of the hospital provided that the staff member is independent of the patient's clinical team.

The inquiry
As soon as possible after the incident has occurred or the suspicion has arisen the investigator will inquire into the allegation. The investigator will act in an inquisitorial capacity and will invite evidence from those making the allegation, from the patient and from any witnesses who the investigator believes will assist in the inquiry. Except in exceptional circumstances the

patient should be present throughout the hearing and should be allowed to put questions to all witnesses either personally or through an advocate.

The finding

If the investigator is satisfied beyond reasonable doubt that the allegation is proved he or she shall make a finding to that effect giving reasons, and both the finding and reasons shall be recorded on the patient's notes. If the investigator is not satisfied beyond reasonable doubt that the allegation is proved but none the less believes that a reasonable suspicion remains he or she may record that suspicion on the patient's notes together with a brief account of the evidence. The record must be shown to the patient who must be offered the opportunity to add comments. In all other cases the fact of the inquiry and the nature of the investigator's finding may be recorded in the notes.

The response

If the investigator is satisfied beyond reasonable doubt that the allegation is proved he or she may award one or more of the disciplinary sanctions listed below. Any sanction must be stated to be of determinate duration, must be recorded on the notes and must be explained to the patient.

In any case where the investigator is satisfied beyond reasonable doubt but does not consider it appropriate to impose a disciplinary sanction, or in any case where the investigator is not satisfied beyond reasonable doubt but considers that a reasonable suspicion remains, he or she may invite the clinical team to propose a therapeutic response to the incident. If the investigator is satisfied that a good case has been made out for the proposed therapeutic response he or she may authorise the response and record that decision and the reasons for it in the clinical notes. In all cases where a therapeutic response is authorised the decision must be fully explained to the patient.

Sanctions
- Loss of all or specific privileges;
- Confinement to the ward;
- Cancellation of trips outside the hospital

In no circumstances may seclusion be used as a disciplinary sanction.

Appeal

In any case where the patient is dissatisfied with either the inquiry process or the nature of the disciplinary sanction imposed he or she must be informed of the right to refer the matter to the hospital complaints procedure at the appropriate level within that procedure.

Publicity
This policy must be displayed in all wards which accommodate detained patients.

Object

The policy accepts that hospital authorities respond to disruptive behaviour on the part of patients and that they are justified in so doing. Its object is to ensure that they do so in a way that is both fair and therapeutic.

Scope

The policy is strictly limited in scope. In the first place, it applies only to detained patients. Secondly it applies to only two categories of behaviour: (a) serious and dangerous behaviour, and (b) behaviour which, although not necessarily criminal, could have a significant impact on the patient's prognosis, discharge, etc. All behaviour in the first category, which includes fire setting and assault, is serious and would amount to a criminal offence. It is therefore entirely appropriate in terms of both the maintenance of order and the safe running of a therapeutic unit for the hospital authority to forbid it. The category should not, however, be extended too far: the demands of order and control should not be over-stretched. Further, it is important to specify the prohibited behaviour with as much clarity and precision as possible (Livingstone & Owen 1983, European Prison Rules 1987).

Included in the second category is behaviour of a highly disturbing nature, such as the possession of pornographic, sadistic or morbid material. While the imposition of a disciplinary sanction might not typically be appropriate in such cases, the behaviour is included in the policy both because of the importance of ensuring the accuracy of any records kept, and because of the need to satisfy the patient that the hospital's response, even if therapeutic rather than punitive, is fair.

Operation

The policy stipulates that no record may be made and no action beyond that immediately required may be taken in any case where a detained patient is suspected of any of the relevant behaviour until an inquiry is held. It is therefore essential that the inquiry process be as quick and simple as possible. If it is seen as unworkable and cumbersome it will be bypassed (HMSO 1991, p. 431).

The nature of the behaviour included in the first category immediately raises the issue of police involvement. If a criminal offence is suspected should not the police be involved? The dilemma is similar, though not identical, to that encountered in the prison context. In prisons the issues of mental disorder and individual responsibility are not so central, but even there the Woolf Report recognised a difference in function between a disciplinary code and the ordinary criminal process: the former is concerned with the maintenance of internal order, while the latter is designed to protect 'the public interest in enforcing and preserving public law and order' (HMSO 1991, p. 427). According to the Woolf Report the disciplinary function could be achieved with the imposition of far less severe sanctions, and the Report recognised that behaviour which was technically criminal might properly be regarded as a disciplinary matter if the level of sanction provided by the disciplinary code was thought to be sufficient. Only where the incident was particularly serious and a criminal sanction thought necessary would reference to the police be essential.

Arguably the arguments for treating incidents internally are equally strong in the hospital context, provided the internal process is acceptable: an internal system will be able to act more swiftly than the police and can be less formal, judgments concerning mental state may frequently be required, and the sanctions available to an internal system can be designed specifically to relate to detained patients. Where a serious offence is suspected, however, it would still be necessary to refer the matter to the police and the hospital authorities would need to develop guidelines to govern such decisions (for the position within the Prison Service see Livingstone & Owen 1993). The relevant factors for consideration might include offence seriousness (HMSO 1992, ch. XXV), the complexity of the investigation required, and the possibility that the patient should be removed from the hospital or have his or her legal status altered, e.g. from section 3 to section 37. In all cases where a reference to the police was made that fact should be recorded in the patient's notes.

Notice

The patient must be informed as soon as possible of the nature of any allegations, and even if the incident is admitted an inquiry into the facts should still be held. It should also be explained to the patient that he or she may be accompanied to the inquiry by an advocate. Since the sanctions available to the inquiry will be relatively minor there would be no right to legal representation under either the common law or the ECHR (*R* v. *Board of Visitors Maze Prison, ex p. Hone* 1988, *Engel* v. *The Netherlands* 1976, *Campbell and Fell* v. *United Kingdom* 1985) and, provided the investigator is properly trained and an advocacy service readily available, there would seem to be no advantage in the introduction of legal representation.

In cases where a reference is made to the police the relationship between the police and the internal investigation would need to be described in the relevant hospital policy. In all cases the hospital must reserve the right to act in the absence of a police decision to charge.

The independent investigator

Since the inquiry process will be dealing with seriously disruptive or disturbing behaviour it is essential that the process be fair and be seen to be so, and that it be such as to produce accurate findings of fact. Independence and impartiality are therefore crucial: they are essential ingredients of procedural fairness (Bayles 1990, Redish & Marshall 1986). Thus in theory the investigator should be entirely independent of the hospital structure but, since it is also required that he or she also be readily available, complete independence is unattainable in practice. However, independence from the clinical team must be achieved. In the more serious cases a statutory hospital manager could act as investigator and could build up considerable expertise over time. In the more routine cases, or where the patient had admitted the incident, an investigator from another clinical team could be appointed.

The inquiry

There is no intention here to suggest that hospitals do not already hold inquiries of some sort. In most, if not all, psychiatric units some investigation will occur in an attempt to establish the facts before any action is taken following a serious incident. However, the fact-finding and decision-making process adopted is typically one of informal discussion between the Responsible Medical Officer and the parties involved (Richardson 1993, ch. 10). Within such a procedure the patient is likely to be at a disadvantage and may be unable to challenge any account provided by the clinical staff. While it is evident that the patient will face considerable difficulties whatever investigative mechanism is adopted – the Ashworth Inquiry for example clearly documents the dismissive attitude often displayed to the evidence of psychiatric patients (HMSO 1992, ch. III) – the informality of current practice renders the patient particularly vulnerable. A more open and participative process is required where the patient is told exactly what is going on, is accompanied by an advocate and has the opportunity to challenge any evidence. It is also important that the investigator act in a fully inquisitorial manner and be trained to guard against any conscious or unconscious bias against the evidence of the patient.

A procedure such as that described should encourage the

accurate finding of fact and should be seen as fair by all concerned including the patient (Bayles 1990, Thibaut & Walker 1975, Lind & Tyler 1988). In its open and participative form it should also be therapeutic and should encourage the patient to take responsibility for his or her behaviour.

The finding

Whatever the underlying cause of the behaviour and whatever the authority's final response to it, it is essential to ensure that the findings of fact be as accurate as possible and be recorded as accurately as possible on the patient's notes. A subsequent reader should be fully informed of what was found and why and what doubts remain. The policy envisages two alternative findings: beyond reasonable doubt and reasonable suspicion. In cases where not even a reasonable suspicion is found the investigator should record the fact of the inquiry on the patient's notes and the negative nature of the finding.

The response

It is not until after the finding of fact that a decision is taken as to the nature of the response. In accordance with other disciplinary schemes be a punitive response should only available when the allegation is established beyond reasonable doubt. However, a beyond reasonable doubt finding would not mandate a punitive response: it would remain open to the authority to respond therapeutically. A therapeutic response would also be permitted where the allegation is not proved beyond reasonable doubt but the investigator is satisfied that a reasonable suspicion remains.

Where a disciplinary sanction is imposed it must be of determinate length. It is punitive and its duration should not be dependent on an improvement in the patient's condition. Where a therapeutic response is authorised great care must be taken to explain everything to the patient, and to ensure that the response is not in effect a covert punishment and is not regarded as such by the patient.

108

Sanctions

The precise nature of the sanctions would vary from unit to unit according to the regime in place and the 'privileges' available. In no circumstances should they include seclusion but they might consist of other forms of restriction or deprivation such as confinement to the ward for a fixed number of days. Whatever the specific nature of the sanctions, however, they must never be such as to reduce the patient's quality of life below an agreed minimum standard. A similar principle is emphasised by the Woolf Report in the context of prison discipline (HMSO 1991, p. 427) and is reflected in Article 3 of the ECHR.

Appeals

It should be open to the patient via the hospital's complaints procedure to 'appeal' against either the investigator's finding or the nature of the disciplinary sanction imposed.

References

BAYLES M. (1990) *Procedural Justice: Allocating to Individuals*. Dordrecht: Kluwer Academic Publishers.

BOYLE A.E. (1994) Sovereignty, accountability and the reform of administrative law. In G. Richardson and H. Genn (eds) *Administrative Law and Government Action*. Oxford: Oxford University Press.

GOSTIN L. (1986) *Mental Health Services: Law and Practice*. London: Shaw and Shaw.

HMSO (1991) *Prison Disturbances April 1990* (the Woolf Report). London: HMSO Cm 1456.

HMSO (1992) *Report of the Committee of Inquiry into Complaints about Ashworth Hospital*. London: HMSO Cm 2028.

HOGGETT B. (1990) *Mental Health Law* 3rd ed. London: Sweet and Maxwell.

LIND E.A. & TYLER T.R. (1988) *The Social Psychology of Procedural Justice*. New York: Plenum Press.

LIVINGSTONE S. & OWEN T. (1993) *Prison Law: Text and Materials*. Oxford: Oxford University Press.

PEAY J. (1989) *Tribunals on Trial*. Oxford: Oxford University Press.

REDISH M. & MARSHALL L. (1986) Adjudicatory independence and the values of procedural due process. *Yale Law Journal* **95** 455.

RICHARDSON G. (1993) *Law, Process and Custody: Prisoners and Patients*. London: Butterworths.

ROSE N. (1985) Unreasonable rights; mental illness and the limits of the law. *Journal of Law and Society* **12** 199.

THIBAUT J. & WALKER L. (1975) *Procedural Justice: A Psychological Analysis*. Hillside New Jersey: Lawrence Erlblaum Associates.

UNSWORTH C. (1987) *The Politics of Mental Health Legislation*. Oxford: Oxford University Press.

Cases

Campbell and Fell v. *United Kingdom* (1985) 7 EHRR 165.
Engel v. *The Netherlands* (1976) 1 EHRR 647.
Pountney v. *Griffiths* [1976] AC 314.
R v. *Board of Visitors Maze Prison, ex p. Hone* [1988] AC 379.

9

Care and Control in the Community

Geoff Shepherd

Introduction

This chapter is concerned with the care and control of people with mental illness who are at risk of committing aggressive or violent acts in the community. It will not deal with the question of whether, and under what circumstances, people with mental illness who are at risk of committing aggressive or violent acts *should* be cared for outside settings like hospitals or secure units – i.e. the question of risk assessment – which is well dealt with in other chapters. Neither will it deal with issues concerned with the merits and demerits of various forms of legal controls in the community (compulsory supervision orders, guardianship powers, etc.). Instead, I will concentrate specifically on the kinds of services that are required and the problems which arise in achieving a good quality of care for this difficult group.

Of course, it may be argued that while *care* in the community is possible – at least in principle – *control* is effectively impossible where the individual is both free in a legal sense and also free in terms of being able to engage with (or avoid) services in a practical sense. However, insofar as it is possible to achieve effective care and control in the community this will depend on: (a) a suitable range of residential and community resources available; (b) clear and widely accepted management procedures; and (c) staff who are not only well motivated to do what can sometimes be a difficult and unrewarding job, but who are also appropriately trained and supported to do so. It is clear that, while an adequate level of resources constitutes a necessary prerequisite of effective care, clear management and good staff training are equally essential. Without them, even the best resourced service will fail. All mental health services ultimately depend on the quality of these interactions between carers – professional or non-professional – and those being cared for and it is in this area that most difficulties arise.

I should also acknowledge at the outset that I approach this topic without a deep knowledge of the problems of mentally ill people who have committed very serious crimes. My clinical background is in the rehabilitation and care of people with severe mental health problems in hospital and in the community and, of course, some of these individuals are, from time to time, aggressive or violent. But, as has been noted by other contributors, very serious attacks in open psychiatric hospitals (and in the community) are relatively rare. Although many patients in rehabilitation services come into contact with the criminal justice system through relatively minor incidents – and here there is a considerable overlap with forensic services – my thoughts regarding community services for those at risk of committing more serious crimes do therefore stem from experience with a slightly different client group. This should be borne in mind when evaluating my remarks.

Current experience with the most difficult patients presenting to general mental health and rehabilitation services suggests that there are essentially two approaches to their care outside hospital.

(1) *Residential care* in some kind of special sheltered accommodation (e.g. 'ward-in-a-house' or 'hospital hostel').

(2) *Intensive community support* from a specialised team of professional workers, perhaps with close collaboration between general mental health services and forensic services.

I will now discuss each of these in turn and describe their strengths and limitations.

112

1. Residential care

For some time now in the general mental health services it has been recognised that there is a small group of patients who do not fit easily into existing services. They are often called 'difficult to place' or are said to exhibit 'challenging behaviour'. Because of the difficulties in finding suitable community placements, they tend to accumulate in hospital units and may also be labelled as 'new' long-stay patients ('new' to delineate them from the 'old' long-stay patients who are currently being resettled as part of the rundown of beds in mental hospitals). These new long-stay patients (difficult to place/challenging behaviour) constitute the most difficult patients currently presenting to mental health services, and within this group there is a significant proportion with histories of aggression and violence. Indeed, it is often these factors which make their community placement problematic.

Regarding their characteristics, the classic paper of Mann & Cree (1976) reported on a national survey of new long-stay (NLS) inpatients (defined as those who had been in hospital continuously for more than one, but less than five, years) and described a population with multiple disabilities, 60% of whom had a diagnosis of psychotic disorder (mostly schizophrenia). They showed severe positive and negative symptoms which were generally highly resistant to treatment, they were socially unskilled, with poor work records, few family ties, and poor physical health. Many also exhibited a range of behavioural problems including violence, self-harm and extreme antisocial behaviour. Nevertheless, about a third were judged to be capable of living in the community if highly supervised hostel placements were available, about a third were deemed to require further treatment in hospital, and the remainder were so multiply handicapped that it was difficult to see where they might be placed. Continuing care in hospital was simply the 'default' option. Several further studies have subsequently appeared of similar samples, both in this country and in the United States, describing similar characteristics (Wykes 1982; Bigelow *et al* 1988; McCreadie & McCannell 1989; O'Driscoll *et al* 1990; Clifford *et al* 1991; Dayson *et al* 1992). As the availability of mental hospital beds has reduced, many of these patients now find themselves caught in the revolving door of multiple, repeated inpatient admissions interspersed with brief periods in the community.

It clear that the number of individuals falling into these categories varies considerably in different parts of the country. Thus, Wykes & Wing (1991) cite evidence from case register data indicating a median prevalence of around 12/100,000 beds occupied for more than one, but less than five, years, but a variation from less than 5/100,000 in Oxford and Worcester, to more than 30/100,000 in Camberwell and Salford. These differences are partly attributable to the influence of adverse social conditions (poverty, poor housing, deprivation, etc.: Thornicroft 1991) and partly to differences in local attitudes towards admission and discharge and the availability of alternative accommodation (e.g. long-stay beds in mental hospitals, supervised hostels in the community, etc.). These variations in prevalence make the planning of adequate service provision difficult and highlight the necessity of local surveys of need.

For some time now the preferred residential option for these patients has been the 'hospital hostel' or 'ward-in-a-house' (Bennett 1980; Wykes 1982). The concept of a 'ward-in-a-house' attempts to combine the best features of high quality hospital care (e.g. high staffing levels, intensive professional input, highly individualised programmes) with a setting that is both homely and domestic in scale and operation (e.g. non-institutional appearance, good access to community facilities, 'normal' expectations of participation in cooking, cleaning, housework, etc.). Most of these units have been located in the community, but near to existing hospital sites. The inquiry team who reported on the care of Christopher Clunis (Ritchie 1994) noted the shortage of such long-term, highly supervised accommodation and recommended the establishment of what they called 'haven' type accommodation to complement acute and secure beds (para. 51.0.9 iv, p. 122). This corresponds closely to the ward-in-a-house model.

Several such projects have now been established, and their progress has been reviewed in Young (1991). The outcome evidence has been reviewed in Shepherd (1991). This suggests that they may be effective in improving the functioning of between 40 and 50% of the NLS such that they are able to be resettled in less highly supervised accommodation in the community, but this can take anything up to five years. However, there is a tendency for most improvement to occur within the first two to three years. (This is consistent with other evidence regarding the rates of movement within this population; see Clifford *et al* 1991.) For those who were not resettled, the units were effective in maintaining social functioning, increasing contact with the community, and producing higher levels of satisfaction compared with matched groups cared for in traditional long-stay wards or acute units in general hospitals. Costs were also generally less than in district general hospital based acute units, but higher than in long-stay wards in mental hospitals (Hyde *et al* 1987). Although such units seemed to be effective for the majority of the NLS, it was noted there was a proportion of patients who did not seem to benefit and they often functioned better in the less demanding setting of a traditional long-stay ward. These individuals tended to show the highest levels of dangerous and 'acting out' behaviour.

In the most recent follow-up study, Shepherd *et al* (1994) examined the characteristics and outcomes of more than sixty referrals of new long-stay/difficult to place patients to two specialised ward-in-a-house facilities in the Cambridge health district over a period of up to seven years. The average age was just under forty, three-fifths were men, 80% had a diagnosis of schizophrenia, and just under three-quarters had been in hospital continuously for more more than six months, but less than five years. In terms of outcomes, 40% were resettled to the community with an average length of admission of just under eighteen months. Approximately one third were transferred, usually following some kind of violent or aggressive incident, after an average length of stay of eighteen months. The remainder were ongoing. King & Shepherd (1994) attempted to analyse the differences between these three groups and found little difference on admission in terms of history, diagnosis or current functioning. However, there were differences in terms of their progress over time. The group who were successfully discharged showed greater evidence of improvement and better functioning around the time of discharge, whereas the 'transferred' group showed more evidence of deterioration in both their mental state and their general functioning. The 'ongoing' group were characterised by slow oscillations in their functioning over long periods of time.

Hospital hostels or ward-in-a-house facilities may therefore provide an effective solution for the majority of new long-stay or difficult to place patients, many of whom also show some degree of aggressive or violent behaviour. It is therefore disappointing to note that in a recent audit of NLS (defined as continuous inpatient admission of more than six months and less than three years) carried out by the Royal College of Psychiatrists research unit, less than 10% of these patients were actually being cared for in such units. The remainder were either in traditional mental hospital wards or stuck on acute admission wards (Lelliot & Wing 1994). This gives an indication of the size of the shortfall regarding specialist residential provision for this group.

Such units are neither cheap nor easy to run, and it requires considerable efforts with regard to staff training and support to maintain good quality care and prevent them from lapsing into institutional practices. Staff tend to find both overt aggressive and 'acting out' behaviour and the more 'negative' symptoms difficult to deal with. Indeed, there is some evidence that it is particularly the negative symptoms (underactivity, lack of motivation, social withdrawal) which are most likely to give rise to critical and hostile reactions on the part of staff (Moore *et al* 1992). This is consistent with the literature on family interactions, where a high 'EE' environment (criticism, hostility, overinvolvement) is very strongly associated with high levels of negative symptoms (Brewin *et al* 1991). In order to counteract these problems staff require intensive 'on the job' training aimed at helping them accurately to identify these behaviours and learn coping strategies to deal with them (Shepherd 1995).

These units are also not a panacea and they seem to experience particular difficulties with those individuals who show the greatest tendency to act out repeatedly in a violent or aggressive manner. (Of course, they may not necessarily be judged the most dangerous.) However, there is a small group who seem to be over-stressed by such environments and eventually act out in such a way that it is felt that they can no longer be managed safely within this kind of setting. It is difficult to identify these individuals *a priori*, but they do appear to show more evidence of deterioration (and less improvement) over time. They may need a higher level of security (e.g. a regional secure or medium secure unit), but they often seem to function better in a less intensive and less socially demanding environment. It may be that they find the interpersonal demands and the physically limited space in these houses very difficult and it is these factors which maintain their psychotic symptoms at relatively high levels, thus reducing their threshold for aggressive or violent behaviour. One possible way around this would be to provide settings (other than long-stay wards in hospital) which provide greater opportunities for privacy and social withdrawal. Small individual flatlets, possibly arranged close to a central staffed hostel on a 'core and cluster' model, would be one possible solution. But they would still require high levels of support and supervision, with staff able to visit regularly during the day and in the evenings and at weekends. The problem of how to provide intensive support, while at the same time not putting too much pressure on people, is one of the fundamental management problems with this group.

2. Intensive community support

This brings us to the question of intensive community support in more 'ordinary' residential settings, without permanent staffing on site. As indicated, this may be a particularly useful option for those who find the demands of living in close proximity with other patients (and staff) too stressful. It may also be more consistent with the expressed wishes of many patients who do not want to be labelled as 'mental patients' and do not wish to live with other mentally ill people, whom they do not know and have not chosen to be with (Carling 1993; Tanzman 1993). These are legitimate wishes and we should strive to take them seriously if for no other reason than that it may help build a good relationship and thereby facilitate compliance with other aspects of care (e.g. medication).

The Ritchie Report discussed the use of specialist community teams in connection with their suggestions regarding the care of what they refer to as 'the special supervision group' (Ritchie 1994, 47.0.5), and many mental health services are now contemplating the creation of specialist teams to look after those placed on the new 'supervision registers'. It is therefore instructive to examine the research which has tried to identify the elements of effective teamworking. Most of this work comes from the literature on 'case management' approaches with the severely mentally ill, and its relevance to mentally disordered offenders has been previously discussed in Shepherd (1993).

Effective teamworking

(a) First, teams need to be clear about their aims and objectives. Most community mental health teams attempt to provide a mixture of extended outpatient support (mainly for people with neurotic disorders), treatment of acute crises (acting as an alternative to inpatient admission where this is feasible), and intensive support for a more disabled population whose needs are primarily *social* rather than *medical*, but who from time to time may go through periods of acute destabilisation. Teams cannot perform all these functions simultaneously and well. They therefore need to be clear about their priorities and have ways of monitoring their workloads so that they ensure they remain on target.

(b) Depending on their objectives, they will then need a particular 'skill mix'. If they are primarily concerned with symptomatic treatment (whether dealing with neurotic disorders or acute psychosis) they will need a highly professionalised team with very good medical and psychological input. However, if they more concerned with delivering social care – as is often the case with the kinds of people we are concerned with today – then they may benefit from the input of non-professionally trained care assistants or support workers who can attend to the patients' practical needs (e.g. shopping, cooking, going to the Post Office, etc.). Of course, such workers will still need good professional supervision, and it should be emphasised that this is not an argument for 'de-professionalising' the service. Given the risks involved, that would be foolish. However, there is a real question regarding the appropriate *balance* between professional and non-professional staff and this can only be resolved by being clear about exactly what range of functions we wish teams to perform.

(c) In terms of the professional input, there is clearly a strong argument for a collaboration between forensic specialists (psychiatrists, nurses, psychologists, etc.) and mainstream mental health professionals. The expertise of forensic colleagues in the ongoing assessment of risk and the management of non-compliance will be of particular value.

(d) Regarding the methods of operation: first, we must define what we mean by intensive support. As a rule of thumb this may be regarded as the ability to provide at least daily visits. It also means that teams must be able to operate on an extended hours basis (i.e. evenings and weekends) preferably with some kind of on call arrangement to provide 24-hour cover. To achieve this intensity of support, teams obviously need to be adequately resourced. The staff involved should be providing more or less full-time commitment so that they can be rostered to provide the out of hours cover. This will require a minimum of six to eight full-time staff; twelve people, each giving a part-time commitment, will simply not be able to provide the cover. Teams also need to have 'limited and protected caseloads' (Ritchie 1994,

47.0.5) and the literature on specialised case management teams which focus on the most severely disabled long-term mentally ill suggests that we should aim for caseloads of less than twenty, preferably less than ten (Ryan *et al* 1991). Finally, staff must practise assertive 'outreach', i.e. they must be prepared to take the service to the client if the client is not prepared to come to the service. This means developing a different attitude to working with unmotivated clients. Staff often find this difficult as it may challenge some fundamental assumptions about the balance between the rights of the individual and the need to exert a degree of control and social pressure. These are difficult ethical and professional isssues, but they have to be addressed (hence the need for good supervision; see (ix) below). If they are resolved, then this approach can engage and maintain contact with some of the most difficult 'at risk' clients, and can even improve outcomes (Cooke *et al* 1994).

(e) At the heart of effective teamworking lie the issues of communication and accountability which are so vividly highlighted in the Ritchie Report. Teams need to be clear not only about what they are supposed to be doing, but also *who* is supposed to be doing it. To achieve this, they need to be effectively *managed* and this is probably the area that needs most attention in current mental health services. I will therefore make a number of separate points concerning teamwork and responsibilities:

Effective team management

(i) Effective team management will probably require some weakening of existing professional line management structures and a corresponding strengthening of operational, 'clinical' management. It thus requires somebody who is administratively and managerially in charge of the team and who has the authority to instruct *all* staff to comply with agreed operational procedures.

(ii) There is no conflict between this kind of clear operational management for the team as a whole and *individual* accountability for specific actions. Within an effective team, each person remains responsible for his or her own actions and must not act negligently or outside that individual sphere of professional competence. These responsibilities cannot be delegated, nor can they be assumed by any one member of the team on behalf of another.

(iii) Except when one member of the team has a designated responsibility to ensure that certain team actions are carried out, no one professional therefore carries ultimate responsibility for the actions of the team. Although certain individuals may have important statutory responsibilities under the Mental Health Act (e.g. psychiatrists or social workers) the concept of ultimate responsibility is actually a myth. There is only the collection of individual responsibilities which go to make up the work of the team. The Clunis Report amply demonstrates this principle, apportioning responsibility across the wide range of staff who came into contact with him.

(iv) One of the key areas of individual responsibility (which cannot be delegated) is to pass on clinically important information regarding the mental state or behaviour of the patient to colleagues in the team, or to outside agencies. Where a specific team member is not able to be present at a particular meeting, it remains his or her responsibility to ensure that important information is communicated using whatever procedures are agreed (e.g. message books, computerised information systems, etc.).

(v) However, because of the likelihood that individuals will be absent from time to time (on holiday, sick, on a training course, etc.) teams should not adhere too strictly to a model of individual responsibility. They must to a certain extent share responsibilities and carry a team accountability for the transmission of information and the performance of certain actions. It should be repeated that there is no conflict between this notion of team accountability and the individual accountabilities carried by each person (which for at least one individual may include aspects of the overall management of the team).

(vi) Team members also need to strike an appropriate balance between the need to preserve confidentiality between themselves and the client, and the need for other professionals – and other agencies – to be aware of certain information. In the case of Christopher Clunis, probably the greatest deficiencies in his care revolved around the failures of staff to pass on information concerning his mental state and behaviour to relevant others. There is clearly a difficult balance to be struck here, but professionals cannot hide behind confidentiality as an excuse for poor communication.

(vii) In order to clarify these different team and individual responsibilities, effective leadership is required. Effective leaders must be able to analyse and structure tasks *and* to commit the team to carrying these tasks out, through a combination of managerial authority and the provision of socio-emotional support. Leaders therefore need both leadership skills and managerial authority to carry out their roles successfully. These attributes are not necessarily associated with one particular profession or discipline, but they can be improved by training and clarification of management processes. Professionals who take on the management of the team must be clear about *both* their authority *and* their responsibilities, since they cannot be held accountable for actions over which they have no authority.

(ix) Teams need effective mechanisms of review, both in terms of their operational procedures and in terms of clinical matters. Teams are not fixed objects; they are continually changing and procedures therefore have to be continually reviewed. Similarly, clients are continually changing and it is the essence of good practice that their care is constantly monitored and adjusted in the light of changing needs and circumstances. This may be done on an individual or group basis, and such supervision must pay particular attention to the dangers of high 'EE' and the counter-transference issues discussed earlier. There is a possible role here for independent advocates to ensure that the patients' needs are really taken into account.

It has to be acknowledged that it is difficult to get teams to work effectively, but unfortunately there is no other solution. The care of individuals with serious mental illness *and* a potential for serious violence is simply too complicated to be carried by one individual. Effective teamwork is the only means whereby the range of necessary skills to address the problems can be brought together. Similarly, good teamwork is the only way that crucial information can be shared and made available in a crisis and that some semblance of continuity of care can be achieved. To be successful, teams have to use *all* the resources available, including the GP and the family. Once again, it was clear in the Clunis case that the family and GPs often had a good idea of what was going on, but the mental health teams failed to involve them appropriately. Finally, we must note that teams will always be restricted by the social conditions and the infrastructure in which they operate. If the person is living in poor housing, with no money, nothing to do, hostile neighbours and no social support, then it will be difficult for a team – no matter how good – to achieve very much. Effective teamworking is central to the success of community care, but it cannot be used as an excuse for not providing basic services.

Conclusions

I have continually referred in this chapter to the care of Christopher Clunis. This is because, in my view, his case reveals almost all the problems of providing good quality effective care in the community for people with mental illness who are also at risk of committing serious aggressive or violent acts. These problems are formidable. At their heart is the fundamental dilemma of where to draw the line between concerns for the liberties and civil rights of the individual patient and concerns for the safety of the public who must be protected from random acts of aggression or violence. If we are to succeed in resolving this dilemma, it will depend on the resources and the quality of the facilities that can be provided and the quality of the staff and the organisation and training that we give them. Effective community care, especially for this client group, will not be cheap, but so far no study of community services has ever found them to be *more* expensive than hospital-based alternatives

(Goldberg 1991). There are therefore community options which are both feasible and effective, but it must be said that at present, in most parts of the country, there is a serious shortage of facilities and staffing and a lack of clear organisation and management. This must change. If we fail to provide adequate care *and* control for this most vulnerable and difficult group, then not only will the public be exposed to unacceptable risk, but also more unfortunate individuals like Christopher Clunis will find themselves living in even more restrictive conditions, for longer periods of time than perhaps is really justified.

References

BENNETT D.H. (1980) The chronic psychiatric patient today. *Journal of the Royal Society of Medicine* **73** 301-3.

BIGELOW D.A., CUTLER D.J., MOORE L.J., McCOMB P. & LEUNG P. (1988) Characteristics of state hospital patients who are hard to place. *Hospital and Community Psychiatry* **39** 181-5.

BREWIN C.R., MACCARTHY B., DUDA K. & VAUGHN C.E. (1991) Attribution and expressed emotion in the relatives of patients with schizophrenia. *Journal of Abnormal Psychology* **100** 546-54.

CARLING P.J. (1993) Housing and supports for persons with mental illness: emerging approaches to research and practice. *Hospital and Community Psychiatry* **44** 439-49.

CLIFFORD P., CHARMAN A., WEBB Y. & BEST S. (1991) Planning for community care: long-stay populations of hospitals scheduled for rundown or closure. *British Journal of Psychiatry* **158** 190-6.

COOKE A., FORD R., THOMPSON T., WHARNE S. & HAINES P. (1994) 'Something to lose': case management for mentally disordered offenders. *Journal of Mental Health* **3** 59-67.

DAYSON D., COOCH C. & THORNICROFT G. (1992) The TAPS project. 16 difficult to place long-term psychiatric patients: risk factors for failure to resettle long-stay patients in community facilities. *British Medical Journal* **305** 993-5.

GOLDBERG D. (1991) Cost-effectiveness studies in the treatment of schizophrenia: a review. *Schizophrenia Bulletin* **17** 421-6.

HYDE C., BRIDGES K., GOLDBERG D., LOWSON K., STERLING C. & FARAGHER B. (1987) The evaluation of a hostel ward: a controlled study using modified cost-benefit analysis. *British Journal of Psychiatry* **151** 805-12.

KING C. & SHEPHERD G. (1994) *Outcomes in Hospital Hostels: A Prelimi-*

nary Search for Predictors. Paper presented at the Ninth Annual TAPS Conference, Royal Free Hospital, London.

LELLIOT P. & WING J.K. (1994) A national audit of new long-stay psychiatric patients. II: Impact on services. *British Journal of Psychiatry* **165** 170-9.

McCREADIE R.G. & McCANNELL E. (1989) The Scottish survey of new chronic in-patients: five-year follow-up. *British Journal of Psychiatry* **155** 348-51.

MANN S. & CREE W. (1976) 'New' long-stay psychiatric patients: a national sample survey of fifteen mental hospitals in England and Wales 1972/73. *Psychological Medicine* **6** 603-16.

MOORE E., KUIPERS L. & BALL R. (1992) Staff-patient relationships in the care of the long-term adult mentally ill – a content analysis of Expressed Emotion interviews. *Social Psychiatry and Psychiatric Epidemiology* **27** 28-34.

O'DRISCOLL C., MARSHALL J. & REED J. (1990) Chronically ill patients in a district general hospital unit: a survey and two-year follow-up in an inner-London health district. *British Journal of Psychiatry* **157** 694-702.

RITCHIE J.H. (Chairman) (1994) *The Report of the Inquiry into the Care and Treatment of Christopher Clunis.* London: HMSO.

RYAN P., FORD R. & CLIFFORD P. (1991) *Case Management and Community Care.* London: RDP Publications.

SHEPHERD G. (1991) Psychiatric rehabilitation for the 1990's. In F.N. Watts & D.H. Bennett (eds). *Theory and Practice of Psychiatric Rehabilitation.* Chichester: Wileys.

SHEPHERD G. (1993) Case management. In W. Watson & A. Grounds (eds). *The Mentally Disordered Offender in an Era of Community Care: New Directions in Provision.* Cambridge: Cambridge University Press.

SHEPHERD G. (1995) Residential care for the severely disabled. *Community Mental Health Journal* (in press).

SHEPHERD G., KING C. & FOWLER D.G. (1994) Outcomes in hospital hostels. *Psychiatric Bulletin* **18** 609-12.

TANZMAN B. (1993) An overview of surveys of mental health consumers' preferences for housing and support services. *Hospital and Community Psychiatry* **44** 450-5.

THORNICROFT G.J. (1991) Social deprivation and rates of treated mental disorder. *British Journal of Psychiatry* **158** 475-84.

WYKES T. (1982) A hostel-ward for 'new' long-stay patients: an evaluative study of a 'ward-in-a-house'. In J.K. Wing (ed.) *Long Term Community Care: Experience in a London Borough.* Psychological Medicine Monograph Supplement 2. Cambridge: Cambridge University Press.

WYKES T. & WING J.K. (1991) 'New' long-stay patients: the nature and size of the problem. In Young, R. (ed.) *Residential Needs of Severely Disabled Psychiatric Patients – The Case for Hospital Hostels.* London: HMSO.

YOUNG R. (1991) *Residential Needs of Severely Disabled Psychiatric Patients – The Case for Hospital Hostels.* London: HMSO.

Response to Violence: A Framework for Fair Treatment

Liz Sayce

Introduction

Homicides by people diagnosed mentally ill have been highly prominent in both public and policy debates in the 1990s. Inquiry teams have investigated the death of Georgina Robinson and the care and treatment of Christopher Clunis, who killed Jonathan Zito (Ritchie 1994). Homicides have also been studied by the Confidential Inquiry into Homicides and Suicides by Mentally Ill people, set up by the Department of Health in 1991, which found a total of 34 such deaths from homicide in a three-year period (Boyd 1994). There is a consensus between service users, professionals and policy makers that all possible lessons from these deaths should be learnt. However, many other tragedies occur which do not receive the same degree of attention: the deaths of psychiatric patients associated with neuroleptic drugs, running at about one a week, or four times the rate of the homicides (MIND 1994); the harassment and sometimes violence perpetrated against users of mental health services; and the continued detention of some people in high security hospitals when they have been assessed as being ready for transfer – with, in 1993, 63 people waiting longer than the six months maximum recommended by the NHS Executive (DOH 1994).

The debate on these matters has become unbalanced. Given the emphasis of most media coverage, the public could reasonably assume that if all those diagnosed schizophrenic took their medication then tragedies could be averted (when in fact the medication in question is implicated in a larger number of deaths than the number of homicides); that violence is committed by service users against non-users, not the other way round (when in fact both occur); and that the main problem of mental health policy is that hospital beds have been so far reduced that people are being discharged unsafely on a significant scale (when in fact the most damaging gap in services is the paucity of community services, which leave some people on acute psychiatric wards only because they are homeless (HMSO 1994); and others unjustly detained in secure hospital provision for longer than needed).

An unbalanced debate carries risks. First, there is a risk that service users could be faced with increasing public intolerance as they are assumed to be potentially (even if not actually) violent – a charge of 'presumed guilty', from which it is virtually impossible to demonstrate innocence. Secondly, there is a risk that policy measures will concentrate on containing this public fear through supervision registers and other methods of control, rather than developing policy which responds to the whole picture of need and the complex pattern of risk. The risks that must be examined include risk to users from violence, from psychiatric treatment and from the trauma of being treated against their will – an act which in any other circumstances would be seen as an assault and which is indeed experienced as assault by service users. It is notable that there has as yet been no confidential inquiry into deaths from neuroleptic drugs: no one knows exactly how often they occur; no one has systematically looked at the lessons that can be learnt; they have received very little attention in the media; and there have been no policy initiatives – equivalent to measures like supervision registers which are supposed to prevent user violence or suicide – to ensure that people are not prescribed dangerous levels or combinations of drugs.

This is not the first time that particular types of tragedy have become the trigger for policy change. In the 1970s the Butler

Committee was set up following a high profile case in which a man who had previously poisoned his family was discharged from Broadmoor Hospital and subsequently offended (Butler 1975). The challenge for mental health policy is to be as much influenced by hopes, aspirations and knowledge of good practice as by tragedies; and as much influenced by tragedies that do not grab public attention as by those that do.

This chapter looks at the whole picture of how violence is an issue for people using psychiatric services; and sets out a framework for action to promote a just response. In concentrating on some of the less widely reported implications of violence for users, there is no intention to play down the significance of the terrible deaths from homicide of Georgina Robinson and others. While there are no simple solutions to the complexities of risk assessment, we need a system that is – and is known to be – 'fair enough'.

Public debate and public perceptions

To quote a user expressing frustration at the constant media assumption that people diagnosed mentally ill are violent:

> I am about as dangerous as a butterfly on valium.

Most people using mental health services are not violent. Yet violence becomes, almost inevitably, a part of their emotional and conceptual world in a way that it does not for everyone else. This is because, violent or not, once diagnosed mentally ill one is faced with the profoundly held association in the public consciousness, between madness and danger. Images of the 'mad axeman' stare back from the pages of newspapers: a Glasgow University study found that two-thirds of media references to mental health related to violence and that these negative images were very likely to receive headline treatment of the 'homicidal maniac' type (Philo *et al* 1993). The assumption that violence and madness are intertwined sometimes suddenly emerges in casual conversation between service users and friends or relatives; indeed the connection has so penetrated people's consciousness that MIND has heard from relatives of people diagnosed mentally ill that they are terrified the individual may become violent – on the grounds that 'it's part of the illness, isn't it?' – even when there is absolutely no evidence of any inclination towards violence:

> Though she has never shown any violent tendencies, how can we be sure what might happen? In the back of my mind is the fear that one day she may harm someone physically. (Meg Henderson (1994) writing of her daughter, diagnosed psychotic.)

Service users are presumed dangerous even when they have never been violent – and therefore have no way to prove themselves innocent. They face this negative image of themselves in the taunts of gangs on street corners, and in organised public lobbies against local mental health centres. To take one example, Gordon Wimbledon, coordinator of a campaign to stop a regional secure unit being set up in Sheffield, was reported as saying: 'No one's going to let children into the valley with lunatics on the loose' (*Sheffield Star* 1993). The campaign included putting posters on trees saying 'Silence of the Lambs'.

When the service user is black the presumption of violence is even stronger: the media concentrates its visual coverage on black perpetrators (such as Christopher Clunis) and white victims (such as Jonathan Zito and his widow, Jayne). The black people who have died do not take on the status of tragic victims: for instance, recent television coverage of deaths associated with neuroleptic drugs portrayed Orville Blackwood as 'highly disturbed' rather than as a young man whose death was simply a tragedy. Photographs of white perpetrators are not shown as incessantly as those of black perpetrators; and when they are the white people are described differently. For instance, the *Daily Express* (1994a), in an article entitled 'Care in crisis as mental patients are freed to kill', used one word under each picture of a person who had killed: under the white faces the words were 'graduate' and 'released'; under the black, 'violent' and 'stabbing'. The stereotype of the 'big, black and dangerous' man is not new (assumptions that black men are more likely to rape, for instance, have been prevalent for centuries: Hoch 1979); but it has recently been powerfully reshaped into the image of the man who is 'big, black, dangerous and mad', an image that has become part of a strong racist undercurrent in public debates on mental health.

There appears to be such a powerful social and psychological investment in the idea of escalating violence by people diagnosed mentally ill, and diminishing control over them, that few people pause to consider the facts. For example, the Interim Report into homicides and suicides in August 1994 (Boyd 1994) found 34 homicides in three years, or about one a month. The press, almost without exception, reported 34 killings in eighteen months under headlines which screamed (quite inaccurately) 'one death a fortnight'. This was partly attributable to an ambiguous press release from the Department of Health, a point which the Department later acknowledged; but even after corrections in the media from, among others, the report's author Dr Boyd, newspapers perpetuated the error: the *Daily Express* (1994b) used '33 cases of violent death in just eighteen months' as evidence of the 'growing toll of people killed by disturbed patients', under the headline 'Tories act over danger patient fear'. The story was prompted by a report by the Mental Health Foundation calling for better funded and co-ordinated community care (Utting 1994): not only was the newspaper distorting this into a story about violence, it also produced copy virtually bound to whip up public fear on the entirely spurious basis that there has been an increase in killings since the introduction of community care. The truth is that there has been no such increase: no increase in killings in the last 30 years and no increase in the last ten years (Home Office 1992; Murphy 1993).

Politicians have joined in what has become a 'moral panic' about increasing violence by psychiatric patients. David Blunkett MP, then Labour's shadow Health Secretary, called for a re-think of the Government's community care policy 'to ensure that all of us can sleep in our beds at night and walk safely in our streets' (quoted in *Western Mail* 1993); and Virginia Bottomley MP, Secretary of State for Health, has used the phrase 'the pendulum has swung too far' (i.e. in favour of civil liberties) – a questionable statement given that compulsory admissions under the Mental Health Act 1983 have increased over recent years (from 16,696 in 1986 to 17,312 in 1989/90) (Hansard 1994); and that there has been no increase in homicides.

At various points mental health professionals, managers and users have attempted to inject some facts into the public debate: for instance, Dr Sandra Grant noted in a letter to the *Independent* (1994) that their article equating having a mental illness with being a highly dangerous criminal was compounding 'the sense of puzzlement and despair that many new patients and their families experience'. But these comments have been almost totally eclipsed by the sheer weight of coverage of what is, in fact, a very small number of killings: 34 in three years, as compared to twelve million people with some psychiatric problems each year and at least 300,000 thought to be 'seriously mentally ill' at any time (Utting 1994). It appears that, irrespective of the facts, the myth of growing patient violence has taken a firm hold: one can only assume that it is serving a function as a focus for social unease and fear of change. In the lives of people in Britain, something feels unpredictable, out of their control. In this climate, people who are different can inspire fear – which gets wrongly interpreted as being a 'realistic' fear of violence. People using psychiatric services have become a useful scapegoat.

While some users respond with strength, mutual support and humour – 'I've got my axe in my handbag' – the reality for some can be a crushing sense of difficulty in being accepted as potential employees, workmates or friends; and in some cases a collapse in self-confidence.

The link between violence and mental health problems: a look at the evidence

Research evidence on the link between 'mental illness' and violent crime is summarised in Chapter 1. The picture is complex but certain points stand out.

10. Response to Violence

The vast majority of people diagnosed mentally ill are not violent. Indeed having a diagnosis of mental illness is not a reliable predictor of violence. Better predictors are: previous violence; use of alcohol; being young and male (Chapter 2). On this data, if policy makers had as their goal the reduction of violent crime (and were not hampered by other political and civil rights considerations), the most effective way forward might be to ban alcohol or to detain young men who had previously committed violence, as a preventive measure. Certainly this would be far more likely to reduce killings than tightening up control over people with mental health problems. It has, however, proved easier to curtail the civil rights of people diagnosed mentally ill than those of many other groups.

However, some people with mental health problems do act violently. The act can, in a minority of cases, be directly associated with the person's mental state: for instance, if someone believes, as part of a delusion, that their only alternatives are to fight someone or to be killed themselves. But more often the violence is independent of the mental health problem. For instance, in 1993 a man who had once had psychiatric treatment mugged an old man in South London. The old man suffered a heart attack and subsequently died. The press covered the story as yet another killing by a psychiatric patient; but there was absolutely no evidence that the man was confused or disturbed when he committed the crime: he happened to be someone who both had had psychiatric treatment and perpetrated a mugging, two facts that were apparently quite independent of one another (*Guardian* 1993).

Evidence on inpatient violence also suggests that violence is often independent of the mental health condition. There is some evidence that inpatient violence is associated with use of illegal drugs and with a previous criminal record; but not with psychiatric diagnosis (Walker & Seifert 1994). It can also be associated with difficult interactions with other people, e.g. racist comments (Powell *et al* 1994).

The assumption in press coverage that psychiatric patients who become violent should not be 'let out' is ethically indefensible in relation to people whose violence is not connected to their mental illness: we do not detain people without mental health problems preventively, on the grounds that they might mug or attack; yet mental health service users are treated as an exception. This issue deserves the widest ethical debate. It is complex given that even where violence *is* linked to a mental health problem, the mental state may be an intervening variable rather than the single cause of violence. For instance, if a person has experienced multiple trauma in childhood, he or she may retreat into 'psychosis' and may be compulsorily detained if there are tendencies to violence. If another person responds to similar trauma by using alcohol and is known regularly to attack people when drunk, this person is not preventively detained.

In almost all cases of violence by mental health service users the person is known to the attacker. Only two out of the 34 cases identified by the Confidential Inquiry involved killing of a stranger. Although the killing of Jonathan Zito by Christopher Clunis – a stranger – has become emblematic of public concern, it is in fact an exceptional case. Much more common are the cases of men killing their wives, girlfriends or mothers, or women killing their children (Boyd 1994). These acts do not necessarily have anything to do with the person's mental health problem. People with mental distress, like anyone else, can become aggressive towards their partners, children – or indeed the strangers with whom they have been placed in close proximity on a psychiatric ward.

The public is quite wrong to believe they are seriously at risk from deranged strangers (the mad axeman stereotype). On the occasions when service users do become violent it is often for a reason, not just through 'madness'. But, once diagnosed mentally ill, it is all too easy for the act to be stripped of its meaning and subsumed in the assumption that 'he (or she) did it because of the illness'. This tendency to explain behaviour in terms of symptoms rather than in terms of the meaning that it has for the individual is not confined to debates in the press; it also seeps into professional attitudes and practice.

The link between violence and mental health problems: professional perceptions and practice

We conclude that Orville Blackwood's violence was the result of a combination of frustration and mental illness .... The handling of a psychotic episode will differ from the handling of normal frustration at being denied liberty. We were not convinced that this difference was always appreciated by the staff treating him. The increasing build up in tension that he displayed following his last Tribunal appearance was not addressed through counselling as we would have expected. It was clear to us that staff were frightened of him; they seemed to perceive his anger and frustration as symptoms of his mental illness (Prins 1993).

Many people tell MIND that within the mental health services they find that they cannot get their anger or frustration taken seriously – it is rather seen as a symptom and treated as such, often with drugs. The individual cannot get away from the supposed link between the 'mental illness' and violence or anger – when in reality the two things may be entirely unconnected. Indeed treating the supposed 'symptom' of anger with drugs – far from preventing violence as is assumed in most public debate – may just store up more anger, if the individual does not have a chance to express the reasons for his or her feelings. In the case of Orville Blackwood there were many sources of frustration: he felt that he should have been discharged from secure hospital provision, because if he had been in prison he would by now have served his time; he was frustrated at not being able to be a father to his children; he objected at times to being placed in seclusion, or having his drug dosage increased. While the Inquiry found the staff did not recognise or address these 'normal' frustrations, other patients seemed to:

We were told [by another patient] that in the past he might ask to be secluded and then come out after a few hours with no problem. But if he felt he was being secluded unfairly he would bang and shout (Prins 1993).

The problem was that once Orville Blackwood became angry he seemed to be treated, for what were seen as symptoms of his illness, more coercively. At times the police were called (in one case in riot gear), at other times he was prescribed higher doses of medication or placed repeatedly in seclusion (solitary confinement). It may be imagined that, if his fellow patient was right that part of his anger stemmed from a sense of injustice, this coercive response would just fuel his anger further, in what could amount to an endless vicious circle. In Mr Blackwood's case the ultimate outcome was his death in seclusion, following the unannounced entry into the seclusion room of between five and seven members of staff; the cause of death was 'cardiac failure associated with the administration of phenothiazine drugs' according to the pathologist's report.

The report into his death (Prins 1993), subtitled 'big black and dangerous', describes how these events occurred in a context in which staff were afraid of a large black patient and had inadequate awareness of issues of race and culture:

> We have described previously a culture within the hospital that is based on white European norms and expectations. As such, there exists a subtle, unconscious on the whole, but nevertheless effective form of organisational racism.

> Ethnic minority patients within the hospital are terrified the authorities are killing them off. This climate of fear among the Afro-Caribbean patients needs to be addressed urgently.

People in psychiatric hospitals, especially those detained compulsorily under the Mental Health Act (MHA) 1983, are under intense scrutiny. When they express violent thoughts or get angry, this can easily be slotted into an interpretation of their pathology. Yet many people outside the psychiatric system get into fights, or have an interest in violent fantasies – for example, the many millions who watch violent films or read violent novels, as well as those who write them:

> I write about things that frighten me. To kill someone must be really profound. It must be amazing. Horrifying (Dennis Cooper 1994).

10. Response to Violence

Once diagnosed mentally ill, and especially once compulsorily detained, one's thoughts and fantasies are judged in a different context from those of others; and any anger – which is likely to be seen as part of symptomatology – may be treated with compulsory medication, solitary confinement (seclusion), or other coercion. This in turn leads to more anger, which leads to more control. Those using the coercion justify it on the grounds of the severe danger and disturbance of the patients. For instance, when Broadmoor Hospital started introducing its policy to reduce seclusion, the Prison Officers' Association (POA) responded with a press release detailing the types of injury suffered by their members (one was said to have had his ear bitten off). The POA's logic was, with such dangerous people, they needed the power to control – a position that has been developed since with the aid of the *Sunday Mirror* (1994) who have argued, under headlines such as 'We pay mad killer to "run" psycho homes', that patients' councils are a threat to security at special hospitals. What this argument signally fails to address is the fact that seclusion is more likely to provoke than to reduce anger and disturbance; and that patients' councils are more likely to strengthen, than to threaten, a sense of patient responsibility and cohesion.

> At its worst the use of seclusion may be seen as a primitive and perhaps punitive response to aggressive or anti-social behaviour, inconsistent with a supposedly caring and therapeutic environment (Special Hospitals Service Authority 1993).

In the case of Orville Blackwood the Inquiry team was clear that because the staff perceived danger from the patients, and because some wanted to promote a custodial rather than therapeutic regime, they 'hyped up' danger and produced a macho culture which did nothing to defuse violence:

> We consider the decision to place Orville Blackwood in seclusion was an over-reaction to a patient unwilling to conform to a rigid, structured regime ... . We accept that patients in Broadmoor Hospital can be dangerous, they can be violent and unpredictable, and nursing staff have a very difficult job to do. But we neverthe-

137

less feel that they tend to place too much emphasis on the potential for violence, almost to the extent that they make it more likely to happen (Prins 1993).

It is not only in secure provision that the hospital regime can trigger inpatient violence: Powell *et al* (1994) found that one of the three most common antecedents to violent incidents at the Maudsley was 'restrictions on patients associated with the routine hospital regime'. Walker and Seifert (1994) found violent incidents in an intensive care unit were more frequent during the week than at weekends, the most likely explanation being that 'weekends tend to be less stressful, with fewer management and medication changes, fewer organised activities, and less staff-patient contact'. Trained staff were more likely to be attacked than untrained, perhaps because trained staff were involved in setting and enforcing limits and administering medication. This suggests that violence is not simply generated from within the person, because of their 'illness'; it occurs in a context, which may include an unwelcome change of medication, or a hospital rule that seems unreasonable to the individual, or (as in the case of Orville Blackwood) a request that he go to occupational therapy when he did not want to go.

Historically institutions developed coercive approaches in a context of policies and practices geared to containing disturbed behaviour and to protecting the public from the mad. 'If a man is mad he shall not be at large in the city', as Plato put it in the fifth century BC (quoted in Porter 1991).

The type of institutions which have been set up to fulfil this function for society have been bedevilled by scandals about dehumanising treatment and even brutality:

> Such has been the low standard of much patient care at Ashworth, that the hospital must be a prime candidate to be included as one of the establishments to be visited in the near future by the Committee for the Prevention of Torture and Inhuman or Degrading Treatment or Punishment (DOH 1992).

Arguably this was allowed to happen in a society which did not demand high standards for the people it chose to fear and reject: indeed certain newspapers still complain that psychiatric patients are treated too well, for instance describing Rampton as a holiday camp where people can get a haircut for only 50 pence. Even in hospitals where real efforts have been made to introduce dignity and respect there is all too often a lack of information and choice. A MIND/Roehampton survey of over 500 people who had been inpatients found that 80% did not think they had been given enough information about their treatment; and 85% had not been offered any choice of services (Rogers *et al* 1993).

There are proven ways out of the vicious circle of 'pathologising' all anger, then controlling it, thus exacerbating it and then controlling it more. Some secure units, such as Reaside (see Chapter 7) appear to be finding that working pro-actively to reduce frustrations and avoid an atmosphere of violence, and using no seclusion, can be effective. Many service users know why they get frustrated: for instance, Christopher Clunis, after his killing of Jonathan Zito, commented on the 'frustration that he was not being involved in the decisions that were being made for him and an absence of planned help towards settling down in a home of his own' (Ritchie 1994). Some people can identify clearly what are the triggers to their aggression: it may be an effect of abruptly ceasing to take medication; it may be that anger is stored up after the indignity of being forcibly medicated; or it may be linked to seeing a particular person with whom there is a difficult relationship, or running out of money, or feeling rejected.

There is an urgent need to spread good practice in working with service users to identify triggers to anger and either to prevent them (where the trigger is unfair treatment that could and should be avoided) or learn ways of dealing with them. Service users who have been violent tell MIND that they want to learn how to stop; they also want to be treated fairly. Anger management courses can help, although one woman commented to MIND that she had been taught only how to suppress anger, not how to deal with it and learn from it.

For good practice to grow a positive policy environment is

needed. Unfortunately the moves to increase control over people in the community – through supervision registers and plans for supervised discharge – are already increasing mistrust among users. Survivors Speak Out, in their evidence to the Health Committee on community supervision registers, pointed out that increased supervision in the community could feed a sense of paranoia, exacerbating distress and destroying trust with professionals (HMSO 1993).

Feelings of 'paranoia' can lead to non-compliance with treatment, and to anger; which may lead to more emphasis on control, to make sure the person is contained and takes his or her treatment; which in turn leads to anger: a repetition of the vicious circle that has long operated in institutions, but this time in the community.

Policy makers, as well as mental health staff, need to recognise that some apparent 'symptoms' are caused by mental health policies and practices. To take another example, MIND has consulted users on their views on acute psychiatric units in general hospitals and found deep dissatisfaction on the grounds of lack of safety, lack of privacy, an over-clinical atmosphere and not enough opportunity to talk about problems (Sayce *et al* 1994). If people in such units behave in a disturbed manner this may be not (or not just) because of their original mental distress, but in reaction to their environment. The trade union UNISON has suggested the 'bulldozer option' for the Edith Morgan Centre, the psychiatric unit in which Georgina Robinson was killed and which has been widely criticised for its design and atmosphere; it is a view which should be seriously assessed.

Users as victims of violence

'I keep looking over my shoulder' was the comment of a user contacting MIND who has experienced harassment and abuse because he is known to be an ex-psychiatric patient. He believes this problem to have increased as a result of publicity about users being violent. And a MINDLINK member remarked: 'I know very few users who haven't been physically or sexually assaulted'.

No one knows how many users of psychiatric services are victims of violence and abuse. No figures are kept on this abuse in the community; nor on violence occurring within psychiatric services. It took a television programme to begin to make public the degree of brutality in Ashworth Hospital. Often people do not report assaults to the police, or to mental health staff, because they are not confident that they will be believed or taken seriously.

For many users violence has been a part of their past. Research suggests that 50% of women and 20% of men who see a psychiatrist have experienced some form of sexual abuse in childhood (Palmer *et al* 1992). Many users have experienced physical abuse in childhood, and/or domestic or other violence in adulthood. In the context of the debate about mental health and violence it is noted that many people who commit acts of abuse or assault have themselves been abused. What is noted less often is that many others who have been abused get abused again and again, sometimes because they have not learnt how to protect themselves: hence, for instance, one of the problems on mixed sex psychiatric wards is that some women can be sexually exploited because they have not learnt that they have a right to, and can, say no.

People's current status as psychiatric patients also makes them vulnerable to abuse and assault. Abusers know that people diagnosed mentally ill will not be believed if they try to complain; and the mentally ill person is easy to make the butt of jokes, bullying and other assault. One man told MIND he had had bricks thrown through his windows following verbal abuse centring on his being a 'nutter'. If the person also has learning difficulties, is black or otherwise different from the majority he or she may face additional victimisation.

These problems arise in the community and also on psychiatric wards, where patients may be abused by other patients, by visitors to the ward or by staff.

A young woman who reported sexual assault on a psychiatric ward and intended to keep out of hospital in future was quoted on Esther Rantzen's *That's Life* (1994) as saying: 'I'd feel safer sleeping on a park bench'. It seems extraordinary that despite widespread objections from women to being on mixed sex wards – one survey of over 100 women found that only 3% wanted to be on a mixed ward – and despite numerous reports of sexual assault and harassment occurring in what should be a safe place, no concerted national action has been taken to ensure that this choice is available (Darton *et al* 1994).

Staff are in positions of great power in relation to their patients. One in 25 psychologists surveyed by Warwick University admitted having sex with a patient. One in four had treated someone who had had sex with a previous therapist (Garrett & Davis 1994). As well as these gross abuses there are humiliations – e.g. the gay man in Ashworth forced to wear a placard saying 'homo'; and there are forced treatments, which from the user's perspective are indistinguishable from assaults.

> I found the imposition of a major tranquillizer, administered against my will in injection form on a number of occasions, very destructive to my self confidence and integrity as a person. There are clear similarities between the experience and accounts I've read of rape – the shame and feeling 'I must have been to blame' (quoted in Cobb 1993).

Holding someone down and injecting them against their will – or stripping off their clothes and placing them in 'seclusion' (solitary confinement) – would, in most circumstances and without the provisions of the MHA 1983, be seen by everyone concerned as an assault. Some people who have had compulsory ECT speak of it as 'torture'. In the long term there is a need for a full review of the use of compulsion under the Mental Health Act 1983; in the short term staff must be aware of the devastating effect that it can have and try to avoid compulsion where other alternatives can be found: for instance, by fostering an environment in which people can express their feelings in a number of safe ways (e.g. through exercise, therapy, talking, feeling heard).

It is extremely difficult for people with a psychiatric diagnosis to get redress when they have been victims.

Too often those carrying out such investigations [of patient com-
plaints] rarely, if ever, appear willing to believe what patients say
about their supposed ill-treatment or improper care (Department
of Health 1992).

MIND hears repeatedly from people who have tried to make a
complaint or report a crime, to no avail. One person who called
the police to report an assault was told that her thoughts of being
attacked were 'part of her delusion': they therefore did not
investigate. People on hospital wards note that the first port of
call to make a complaint is the nurses' station – but it may be
the nursing staff whom they want to report for assault; if the
police are called people have found they usually 'take the part of
the nurses'. Not surprisingly MIND hears from many people who
do not bother to pursue complaints at all, for fear of being
disbelieved or victimised, or because there is not an atmosphere
which makes it easy to speak out:

I was pinned down on my hospital bed by a male patient during
the day. He kept following me around. I didn't tell staff because
I had been abused before and felt it was all my fault (user in
Southampton, during the MIND Stress on Women campaign).

MIND's Stress on Women campaign revealed some cases where
assaults on psychiatric wards had been investigated by the
police; but the Crown Prosecution Service had decided not to
proceed on the grounds that the chances of the individual being
believed were too slim. The law itself institutionalises the refusal to believe psychiatric patients. Following prosecution of a
number of Rampton staff, the House of Lords ruled in 1986 that
juries should be warned about the danger of prosecuting staff on
the unsupported evidence of a single patient; and noted that
special hospital patients were 'all persons of bad character
suffering from some form of mental disorder ... and may of
course have all conspired to make false allegations' (*R* v. *Spencer*
1987). This confident statement was made despite the fact that
special hospital patients include people who have committed no
crime at all.

On the rare occasions when people do pursue complaints the experience can be very difficult. For instance, one woman user who complained of sexual abuse by a GP was faced with a General Medical Council panel of twelve men and one woman. Her entire sexual history was brought up, quite irrelevantly. After the doctor was found not guilty of the alleged abuse *GP Magazine* (1993) ran a story under the headline 'GP tortured' detailing the trauma faced by the doctor. There was no mention of the trauma experienced by the woman.

Because so few people with mental health problems make complaints within the NHS about assaults, or report crimes of assault to the police; and because when they do they often do not get very far since the case may 'only' rest on the testimony of psychiatric patient(s), there are no decent statistics on the extent of assault against service users. The problem is still largely hidden.

Conclusion: towards citizenship

There is a common thread in the experiences of people who are falsely assumed to be violent, of those whose violence is wrongly understood only in terms of 'symptoms', and of those who are victims: a lack of status to be believed and taken seriously and a lack of say in what should happen, what would help. MIND believes that violence can be kept to a minimum, and dealt with most effectively, in a system which is designed first and foremost to be fair.

Unfair treatment – by the media, by mental health workers, by members of the public – is wrong *per se* and can make people angry, which all too often leads to more unfair treatment. Users do not want to be assumed guilty of potential violence. They do not want to be 'punished' unfairly. They want sources of anger and frustration to be understood: for instance, the feelings engendered by living in a society that ostracises you once you have a psychiatric history and gives you little chance to find work or a place in the world.

There is, however, no simple consensus about what is 'fair'. A professional administering compulsory treatment following an outburst may believe this is a fair response, since the treatment has been prescribed for the particular individual's illness, it is effective when someone is especially agitated, and it is being administered in accordance with the law. The individual, however, may see things quite differently: he or she may have become angry for very specific reasons, feel no one is listening to the issues and that compulsory treatment is just a way of shutting him or her up.

The staff view of what is fair has the backing of scientific discourse, professional training and the practice of the institution. The user's view can easily be 'pathologised' in a power dynamic which can write out the user's perspective – a fact reputedly noted by a psychiatric patient as long ago as the sixteenth century:

> They called me mad, and I called them mad, and damn them they outvoted me (Nathaniel Lee, quoted in Porter 1991).

The system can only be fair if the user has the opportunity to surprise the worker by revealing a different interpretation of things, just as the staff member may show the user a different perspective. The relationship needs to become more equal: the user must sometimes be able to 'outvote' the staff member, because, as in any dialogue between two adults, sometimes one may have more of value to say on an issue, sometimes the other. Users need more power: not the power to commit violence, but the power to be assumed innocent – by the media, by professionals – unless 'proved' otherwise; the power to be heard when they have been victims; and the power to have a say in explaining why they may get violent and what would help. This is an infinitely more promising way forward than reacting punitively after someone has become violent.

This change in power dynamics can only work with some major changes in practice; and some changes in policy and in the climate of opinion. The following framework for change provides a starting point:

(1) An open debate on the rights of service users in relation to diversion from custody. Orville Blackwood felt that it was unfair that he was still detained after 'serving his time' as he saw it. Especially when people are diverted into secure provision at an early stage, when they have not been found guilty of an offence, there are serious user rights issues which need to be addressed: for instance, the right to have allegations of violence tried and proved.

(2) A thorough review of the MHA, including a full ethical debate on provisions for compulsory treatment. Users experience it as assault; for up to three months drug treatment can be administered without a second opinion, a cut-off point which seems strangely arbitrary. Even with a further opinion the second opinion usually accords with the first; the second opinion process needs to be broadened to include other perspectives as well as medical.

(3) User involvement in all mental health services, to build up a system in which people have a say, not only at critical times, such as Mental Health Review Tribunals, but routinely. Involvement must include opportunities for groups of users to meet, raise issues and be heard. Specific groups may need to meet: for instance, if black men are seen as 'big black and dangerous' or if women are experiencing sexual harassment in a hospital, they may only be able to talk about such issues in black-only or women-only groups.

(4) A chance for individuals to be fully involved in planning their own care. Christopher Clunis commented that he had not felt informed or involved; this is a common complaint. Care planning can include looking at how to avoid being victimised or made a scapegoat; or how to tackle issues that may be making the person angry.

(5) Independent advocacy, to assist the individual in getting a fair deal from the system.

(6) Well publicised and effective complaints procedures (see for instance the MIND/Law Society response (1994) to the Wilson Committee proposals on complaints).

(7) Training for professionals which emphasises the meaning

of experiences that users have and actively discourages seeing behaviour primarily in terms of symptoms. Professionals need to hear direct from service users on these issues in their training.

(8) Research on users' experiences of being victims of violence; of being wrongly perceived as violent; and of being violent, including their perceptions of the underlying causes, the trigger factors, the measures that might have helped and their own ability to predict violence. These issues are all currently under-researched.

(9) Concerted health promotion work, building on the Health of the Nation work already in progress; and work with journalists to counter the inaccuracies and limited vision prevalent in much media coverage of mental health and violence.

(10) A serious re-think of those aspects of current mental health policy which encourage increased coercion in community care, notably guidance on supervision registers and proposals for supervised discharge. There is a real risk that the vicious circle that we have seen in the most problematic institutional practice – where control sparks patients' anger and anger leads to more control – could be repeated in the community.

For this 'alternative ten-point plan' to be implemented requires a shift in social attitudes and in the demands that are placed on psychiatric services. Rather than being expected by the public just to contain madness, the services need to be expected to treat people as citizens. That means that every death of a service user taking neuroleptic medication would assume exactly the same significance as the death of a non-user; if the death rate of one person a week would be unacceptable in maternity or paediatric services, then it should be equally concerning in psychiatry.

We seem some way from this set of attitudes. By and large the public seems unaware of the deaths of Munir Yusuf Majothi, Joseph Watts, Orville Blackwood, Bryan Marsh and the other users who have died.

> I recognise that there have been a number of deaths of psychiatric patients associated with the taking of psychiatric drugs. I accept that these deaths are just as tragic for everyone involved as the

147

homicides and suicides being considered by the Confidential Inquiry (Virginia Bottomley MP, letter to MIND, September 1994).

There is a need for Government to build on this commitment and ensure that social policies build on positive practice; and that where they are addressing the avoidance of tragedy they address all types of potential tragedy. If policy is formed as a response to public fear that mentally ill people are 'out of control' and increasingly killing people in the community – or, worse, if policy adds to that view by including measures to correct a supposed, but uncorroborated, 'swing of the pendulum' in favour of civil liberties – then we shall end up with a policy that is distorted in favour of control of users. It will be a system that is unjust, in that it will not give sufficient weight to users' rightful demands to be treated as citizens. It will lead to vicious circles of control, and then anger and non-compliance, and then more control. It will not end well.

There is an alternative, building on user involvement to create virtuous circles in which users have their own powerfully negative experiences of violence taken seriously, and in which staff feel less threatened, exercise less coercive methods and are met with less anger and resistance. This method is working today in some mental health settings. In Birmingham a home treatment service found that when people knew they were unlikely to be admitted to hospital they were more likely to stay in touch with the service (Dean *et al* 1993); if people do not fear coercion they are also more likely to talk openly and to get more out of the service offered. For good practice to be generalised we need a climate of policy and public opinion in which it can flourish; a climate in which the hold that myths of violence and mental illness have over people can gradually be reduced.

At present Britain is in the throes of a moral panic about mental health service users and violence. That is why any serious look at the issue has to address the question of violence against users and wrongful assumptions about their violence as well as giving users a say in how to prevent user violence. Otherwise well-intentioned examinations of user violence will only add to the distortion in the public debate – which will add to unfairness and set up new vicious circles in which users feel threatened and angry, and are met with ever more control.

This can and must be avoided.

References

BOYD W.D. (Director) (1994) *A Preliminary Report on Homicide.* London: Steering Committee of the Confidential Inquiry into Homicides and Suicides by Mentally Ill People.

BUTLER (Chairman) (1975) *Report of the Committee on Mentally Abnormal Offenders.* London: HMSO.

COBB A. (1993) *Safe and Effective?* London: MIND.

COOPER D. (1994) *Observer* 25 September.

Daily Express (1994a) Care in crisis as mental patients are freed to kill. 22 September.

Daily Express (1994b) Tories act over danger patient fears. 9 September.

DARTON K., GORMAN J. & SAYCE L. (1994) *Eve Fights Back.* London: MIND

DEAN C., PHILLIPS J., GADD E.M., JOSEPH M. & ENGLAND S. (1993) Comparison of community based service with hospital based service for people with acute, severe psychiatric illness. *British Medical Journal* **308** 473-6

DOH (1992) *Report of the Committee of Inquiry into Complaints about Ashworth Hospital.* Cm 2028-1. London: HMSO.

DOH (1994) *Report of the Working Group on High Security and Related Psychiatric Provision.* London: Department of Health.

GARRETT T. & DAVIS J. (1994) Epidemiology in the UK. In JEHU D. (ed.) *Patients as Victims.* Chichester: John Wiley & Sons.

GP Magazine (1993) GP tortured. 23 July.

Guardian (1993) Family irate as killer is freed. 17 July.

Hansard (1994) Written answers, 11 February.

HENDERSON M. (1994) *Guardian* 20 August.

HMSO (1993) *House of Commons Health Committee (1993) 5th Report, Community Supervision Orders.* London: HMSO.

HMSO (1994) Evidence of Joint Forum on Mental Health and Homelessness. In House of Commons Health Committee Report, *Better Off in the Community? The Case of People Who are Seriously Mentally Ill. vol. II Minutes of Evidence.* London: HMSO.

HOCH P. (1979) *White Hero Black Beast.* London: Pluto Press.

HOME OFFICE (1992) *Criminal Statistics England and Wales.* London: HMSO.

Independent (1994) 1 April.

LAW SOCIETY & MIND (1994) *Being Heard. Response to the Report of* the *Wilson Review Committee on NHS Complaints Procedures*. London: MIND.

MENTAL HEALTH FOUNDATION (1993) *Mental Illness: The Fundamental Facts*. London: The Mental Health Foundation.

MIND (1994) *Report on Deaths Caused by Neuroleptic Drugs*. London: MIND.

MURPHY E. (1993) Could do better. *Care Weekly* 18 November.

PALMER R., CHALONER D. & OPPENHEIMER R. (1992) Childhood sexual experiences with adults reported by female patients. *British Journal of Psychiatry* **160** 261-5.

PHILO G., HENDERSON L. & McLAUGHLIN G. (1993) *Mass Media Representation of Mental Health/Illness: Report for Health Education Board for Scotland*. Glasgow: Glasgow University Media Group.

PORTER R. (ed.) (1991) *The Faber Book of Madness*. London: Faber & Faber.

POWELL G., CAAN W. & CROWE M. (1994) What events precede violent incidents in psychiatric hospitals? *British Journal of Psychiatry* **165** 107-12.

PRINS H. (Chairman) (1993) *Report of the Committee of Inquiry into the Death in Broadmoor Hospital of Orville Blackwood and a Review of the Deaths of Two Other Afro-Caribbean Patients. 'Big, Black and Dangerous?'* London: SHSA

RITCHIE J.H. (Chairman) (1994) *The Report of the Inquiry into the Care and Treatment of Christopher Clunis*. London: HMSO.

ROGERS A., PILGRIM D. & LACEY R. (1993) *Experiencing Psychiatry*. London: MIND/Macmillan.

SAYCE L., CHRISTIE Y., COBB A. & SLADE M. (1994) Users' perspective on emergency needs. In Phelan, Thornicroft & Strathdee (eds) *Emergency Mental Health Services in the Community*. Cambridge: CUP.

Sheffield Star (1993) No one's going to let children into the valley while lunatics are on the loose. 8 September.

SPECIAL HOSPITALS SERVICE AUTHORITY (1993) *The Use of Seclusion and the Alternative Management of Disturbed Behaviour within the Special Hospitals*. London: SHSA.

Sunday Mirror (1994) We pay mad killer to 'run' psycho home. 14 August.

UTTING W. (Chairman) (1994) *Creating Community Care. Report of the Mental Health Foundation Inquiry into Community Care for People with Severe Mental Illness*. London: The Mental Health Foundation.

WALKER Z. & SEIFERT R. (1994) Violent incidents in a psychiatric intensive care unit. *British Journal of Psychiatry* **164** 826-8.

Western Mail (1993) 17 July.

Case

R v. *Spencer and others* (1987) AC 128, 137.

Appendix A

Assessing potentially violent patients [N.H.S. EXECUTIVE (1994) *Guidance on the Discharge of Mentally Disordered People and their Continuing Care in the Community*. H.S.G.(94)27. London: Department of Health, Paras 27 & 28]

Patients who have a history of aggressive and risk-taking behaviour present special problems and require very careful assessment. They pose particular challenges to clinicians who have to try to predict their future behaviour and the risks of further violence.

It is widely agreed that assessing risk of a patient acting in an aggressive or violent way at some time in the future is at best an inexact science. But there are some ways in which uncertainty may be reduced:

(a) Making sure relevant information is available

A proper assessment cannot be made in the absence of information about a patient's background, present mental state and social functioning and also his or her past behaviour. It is essential to take account of all relevant information, whatever its source. As well as the treatment team and the patient, sources may include relatives, carers, friends, the police, probation officers, housing departments, and social workers, and also local press reports and concern expressed by neighbours. Proper regard must be paid to legal and other obligations relating to confidentiality. However, wherever possible, information that is relevant to forming an overall view of a case should be made available in the interests of the patient. Too often it has proved

151

that information indicating an increased risk existed but had not been communicated and acted upon.

(b) Conducting a full assessment of risk

The Panel of Inquiry into the case of Kim Kirkham concluded that the following all played a part in arriving a decission about risk:

- past history of the patient;
- self-reporting of the patient at interview;
- observation of the behaviour and mental state;
- discrepancies between what is reported and what is observed;
- psychological* and, if appropriate, physiological tests;
- statistics derived from studies of related cases;
- prediction indicators derived from research.

In the words of the panel:

> The decision on risk is made when all these strands come together in what is known as 'clinical judgement', a balanced summary of prediction derived from knowledge of the individual, the present circumstances and what is known about the disorder from which he [or she] suffers.

It is particularly important to know about the past history of risk-taking and dangerous behaviour. As the Kim Kirkham panel again noted: 'Nothing predicts behaviour like behaviour.'

(c) Defining situations and circumstances known to present increased risk

While judgements about future overall risk posed by individual patients can be difficult, research has indicated that there are particular situations and circumstances which may indicate an

---

* by a chartered psychologist or under the supervision of one.

increased level of risk. For instance, one American study of over 10,000 respondents showed that violence was reported more often when drug or alcohol misuse co-exist with a major mental disorder or when a patient has multiple psychiatric diagnoses.

It is often possible to identify circumstances under which, based on past experience, it is likely that an individual will present increased risk; to indicate what must change to reduce this risk; to propose how these changes might be brought about and to comment on the likelihood of interventions successfully reducing risk.

Some examples are as follows:

- when a patient stops medication;
- when a person who has previously offended under the influence of alcohol or drugs starts drinking again or enters an environment where drugs are commonly availiable;
- when a patient whose aggression has been apparent in one particular situation, e.g. in the context of a close relationship, enters another such relationship.

(d) Seeking expert help

There is a considerable body of expertise on risk assessment within forensic psychiatry. Expert forensic help should always be used in difficult or doubtful cases.

An effective risk assessment will identify relevant factors involved in past behaviour, indicate the circumstances which may influence a patient's tendency to violence in the future and estimate the likelihood of these recurring. All members of the multidisciplinary team and the patient's formal or informal carers will need to be aware of the results of the assessment. Prompt action must be taken in response to any evidence of increased risk.

Appendix B

Check list of points considered by the Home Office in examining cases of restricted patients [The Home Office]

(1) Has any information come to light since the last report which increases understanding of the circumstances surrounding the index offence?

(2) Is the motivation for behaviour that has put others at risk understood?

(3) Is there any evidence that the patient has a persistent pre-occupation with a particular type of violent/sexual/arsonist activity?

(4) What are the chances of circumstances similar to those surrounding the offence arising again and similar offences occurring?

(5) In cases of mental illness, what effects have any prescribed drugs had? Do any symptoms remain? How important is medication for continued stability? Has stability been maintained in differing circumstances? Does the patient have insight into the need for medication?

(6) In cases of mental impairment, has the patient benefited from training? Is the patient's behaviour more socially acceptable? Is the patient explosive or compulsive?

(7) In cases of psychopathic disorder, is the patient now more mature, predictable and concerned about others? Is he more tolerant of frustration and stress? Does he now take into account the consequences for his actions? Does he learn from experience?

(8) Does the patient now have a greater insight into his condition? Is he more realistic and reliable?

(9) Have alcohol or drugs affected the patient in the past? Did either contribute towards his offence?

(10) How has the patient responded to stressful situations in the hospital in the past and how does he respond now – with physical aggression or verbal aggression?

(11) If the patient is a sex offender, has he shown in the hospital an undesirable interest in the type of person he has previously been known to favour as his victim? What form has any sexual activity taken? What have been the results of psychological tests?

(12) What views do members of the clinical team have about the patient's continuing dangerousness?

(13) Is it considered that the patient should/should not continue to be detained? For what reasons?

(14) If so, is it considered that detention in conditions of special security is necessary?

Index